Screwtape:
Letters on Alcohol

Ira W. Hutchison

Sheed & Ward

Sheed & Ward™ is a service of The National Catholic Reporter Publishing Company.

Library of Congress Cataloguing in Publication Data
Hutchison, Ira W.
    Screwtape--letters on alcohol / Ira W. Hutchison.
      p.   cm.
    ISBN 1-55612-565-8 (acid-free paper)
    1. Alcoholism. 2. Alcoholism--Religious aspects--Christianity.
I. Title.
HV5068.H887   1992
362.29'2--dc20   92-18606
                                                  CIP

Published by: Sheed & Ward
                    115 E. Armour Blvd.
                    P.O. Box 419492
                    Kansas City, MO 64141-6492

To order, call: (800) 333-7373

Contents

Preface v
Letter 1 1
Letter 2 5
Letter 3 9
Letter 4 12
Letter 5 15
Letter 6 19
Letter 7 23
Letter 8 26
Letter 9 30
Letter 10 34
Letter 11 38
Letter 12 42
Letter 13 45
Letter 14 48
Letter 15 51
Letter 16 54
Letter 17 58
Letter 18 62
Letter 19 66
Letter 20 69
Letter 21 73
Letter 22 76
Letter 23 80
Letter 24 84
Letter 25 88
Letter 26 92
Letter 27 96
Letter 28 100
Letter 29 103
Letter 30 106
Letter 31 109
Letter 32 113
Letter 33 117
Epilogue 120

To
my families:

of birth
of marriage
of faith
of recovery

and, most of all,

to
Light

Preface

THIS BOOK IS ABOUT STRUGGLE AND SPIRITUAL COMBAT. MORE precisely, the letters within involve people who struggle with the effects of alcohol in their lives, normal mortals whose drinking causes problems for them or for those who love them. The letters are written from a "devil's" point of view; each focuses in some way on an aspect of drinking, the thinking or feeling effects of the disease of alcoholism, or recovery. The writing is snide, greedy and often strident, as might be expected from such a source. The purpose of each of the letters is instructive, with a single goal: to block or destroy any healthy personal development or spiritual growth.

The inspiration for this book is C.S. Lewis' masterpiece, *The Screwtape Letters*, originally published in 1942 and continually reprinted ever since. It is one of Lewis' finest works and an intriguing blend of religion, philosophy and psychology. It was only a chance (so I thought) gift from my sister that *The Screwtape Letters* first came into my hands. This work led me, initially, to be appreciative, then enthusiastic and finally awed, by Lewis' many works. His writing has had a profound impact on my thinking about God, joy, pain, spiritual growth, friendship, love, and miracles. If Lewis were still alive, I believe that he would disclaim any special wisdom; nonetheless, I attribute to him extraordinary insights into the relationship between creation and Creator.

In this book I have attempted to be faithful to Lewis' form and style. If one would learn from a master, I happily urge any reader to lay this gently back on the bookshelf and go and settle in with *The Screwtape Letters*. It is an important work. In his book, Lewis addresses himself to the general dissolution of the human spirit through the weaning away from God. The focus here is more specific. In this series of letters, the focal point is on the struggle with alcohol, most often in the form of alcoholism and its effects.

This book follows Lewis' design, instructional letters from a senior devil, Screwtape, to a junior devil, Wormwood. His characters were so named in order to sound nasty, as explained in a preface he wrote in 1960 for a revised edition. In this work, my junior devil is named Rotbranch, a deliberate image contrived from the Christian tradition which teaches that "God is the vine and we are the branches." The idea of rot is straightforward in all its variations: decaying, corrupting, spoiling, disintegrating. Devil, in whatever theological or religious form the reader wishes to envision, has the purpose of rotting the branches, since He (the devil's enemy) is unassailable. I would not wish to summarize Lewis' conception of devil but it, too, may be found in the preface to his book. He explains his imagery of devils, part of which is that they are motivated by fear of punishment and by a kind of hunger. These letters on alcohol make use of the latter part of the conception and allude to the feasting which devils might make on the human spirit through various types of affliction. Although this is only imagery it is, perhaps, not too strange. How often do we speak of something "eating away at us," or of having a "gnawing feeling"?

Despite an inner cringe, I have retained from *The Screwtape Letters* the reference to God, by Screwtape, as the *Enemy*; I have also borrowed Lewis' reference to Screwtape's boss as *Our Father Below*. These references may cause some readers discomfort; from a "devil's" point of view they are ap-

propriate. Other readers may be unsettled that I have chosen
to retain the convention of using the reference "He" when referring to God. The choice is for literary ease rather than theological precision since God is unlimited by the words we use.
To any readers who would have preferred a gender-free desig-
nation, I sympathetically encourage you to adjust the terms to
fit your heart.

A major difference between the two works lies in the
characters. Lewis primarily followed the bedevilment of one
man through his series of letters. The letters here have many
characters: both men and women, those who are still in the
grips of alcohol and those who are in recovery, those who are
in despair and those who are in hope. The first letters deal
more with active alcoholism, the latter more with the paths of
recovery.

Readers will find herein ordinary women and men, and no
heroes save that we can all be heroes. There is no literary plot
to discern, nothing in particular to connect one person to another. There is nonetheless a plot, simple and timeless: the
gradual, deliberate, and cunning effort to separate the human
spirit from God. Being neither theologian nor wise man, I offer
no speculation about the origin of evil. Any who struggle with
a life problem and to be more open to the love of God can at-
test to a sense of spiritual warfare. To paraphrase St. Paul,
"that which I would do, I do not; that which I would do not, I
do." In such warfare, it does seem as if we are embattled,
gnawed and led away from that which is Good. This book is
simply about those who are embattled in some way by the effects of drinking.

Malediction

"Goad their resentment
toward things they cannot change,
fear of changing the things they can,
and blindness so they see no difference."

—Excerpted from the remarks
of Screwtape, Senior Archdevil,
to the graduating class of devils,
20th Century

Letter 1

Dear Rotbranch,

    It was a great disappointment to me to learn that you had already departed to your assignment prior to my return. It was my intention to have a few private words with my favorite protégé after my speech to your graduating class. My pleasure at such events is beyond description. I can almost taste the decay and corruption you will produce as you begin your assignments on earth.

    As you may have heard, I was called away with some urgency to directly manage the potential failure of an iniquity long in planning. Many of our efforts among mortals are little more than whims, devilish delights for our own amusement and appetite. However, the particular evil to which I was called was in the category of long-term dissolution; its failure would have meant the undoing of many years' work by your colleagues. I am happy to say, although this will come as no surprise to those who know me, that I was quickly able to counter the potential threat. Goodness is most easily vanquished when it is fresh in bloom, before it has had much experience of His damnable light. Good men could have thwarted me but they chose to do nothing. Another easy triumph, but it could have been otherwise. It is well for you to remember that just as we can disrupt the Enemy's plan, He, too, can disrupt ours, and it is never wise to take any of our successes for granted when His souls are involved.

I am pleased that you received your assignment to the alcohol sector with such malicious enthusiasm. It was made clear to you by my assistant that you would be working mainly with mortals having alcohol problems, and with the myriad lives they touch. Some of your clients will be alcoholics, some will be alcohol-dependent, some will be family members. Countless opportunities await you to interfere with their relationships with the Creator, and to lead them ever closer to Our Father Below. I think that you will find the possibility of temptations quite exciting and filling. There will be great diversity in the souls entrusted to your bedevilment but all will have in common some struggle with alcohol—in themselves or those close to them. I am confident that you will not fail to bring many of them into our darkness.

Yours is not an easy century in which to begin your work. On the one hand, your work is made easier by the near universal availability and inexpensiveness of alcohol on earth. Many of your predecessors have devoted their pernicious energies helping to create cultural values which encourage drinking for virtually any occasion, rather than just to celebrate special moments. Indeed, among many peoples, it is now considered a major social blunder to fail to offer guests alcohol immediately upon their arrival. We have also been successful in creating a milieu in many cultures where abstaining is seen as a bit odd. If you can believe this, we have even helped to shape some subcultures where excessive drinking is a source of pride to those who participate, despite the fact that it makes many quite ill! Our devils have, over the centuries, taken a good thing and carefully nurtured the human propensity for excess to our advantage in the destruction of souls. Some of the mortals believe that alcohol is innately evil, although there are fewer and fewer of this sort around. You and I both know that anything which comes from Him is good, but that humans can (with our help, of course) make it otherwise. Your job is to draw out the worst from peoples' use of alcohol, and I believe that you are prepared for the task. It should not be all that difficult.

On the other hand, the 20th century has had certain ominous developments which make our job more arduous, and you need to be reminded of these lest you underestimate your assignment and fail to lead people away from the Enemy. For centuries there was no danger that humans would discover the truth of alcoholism; their ignorance worked greatly to our advantage. God's reasons are never known to us. We can only speculate why His cursed Goodness decided to allow mortals to have the knowledge of the truth that alcoholism is a *disease*. You know that He lets them make these discoveries from time to time as He leads them out of ignorance. I remember how much fun it was when humans believed that the mentally ill were possessed by us! That one kept us amused for centuries.

We had much more room to work our way when everyone believed that those with alcohol problems simply had no will power and were therefore bad people. Now that they know that alcoholism is a disease rather than a moral weakness, they are finding ever-increasing ways to counter the effects. We had not foreseen that they would be given this knowledge and, I must admit, were unprepared for the speed with which such knowledge has led to more discoveries about the biochemistry of alcoholism. True knowledge is always dangerous to our goals and must be thwarted whenever possible. They have even discovered that the brains of those with the disease produce a different chemical response to alcohol than do the brains of other people not so afflicted.

Most dangerous to our efforts are the recovery programs begun by these mortals, particularly AA. His Love has not only given them a truth, He has also provided a way to make use of their disease in bringing them closer to Him through sharing with others.

I cannot overemphasize the importance of counteracting this. Our whole purpose is to decay their connection with the Enemy. He is ever ready to help them in their struggles; we must be ever ready to lead them away. All human characteristics are at your disposal—distort them well.

Sincerely,
Screwtape

Letter 2

Dear Rotbranch,

Your recent reports indicate a certain laziness in pursuing new courses for our consumption. While you have done reasonably well with those specific souls assigned to you, your efforts to control new mortals are not worthy of a devil in training. It is my strong recommendation to you to pursue men and women who are prone to think that they are beyond our grasp. The well-educated and employed, particularly if they are churchgoers, would be a lush menu. Your training should have prepared you to devour this type, but I shall nonetheless take my valuable time to refresh your memory.

Denial is one of the strongest weapons in our arsenal, and with it you can preserve an alcoholic in misery for many, many years. It is not that they are consciously lying to themselves, they simply are unable to admit to the truth that their drinking is more and more out of their control. Where they once enjoyed and were able to control their drinking, the alcohol is now more and more in control of them. The disease suits our purposes best if we can help maintain their denial as long as possible. In this respect, those with major alcohol problems are just like all humans who deny the hard and painful truths about themselves because they are unable (they think) to survive the truth. One of theirs once said that knowing the truth would make them free, and indeed it does. Fortunately for us, we can assist their fears by making the truth intolerable to them. Let them ignore the evidence that their drinking is taking over their lives. Help them to find convenient rationalizations for why they are drinking: good news, bad news, almost anything will do. If you sustain the right balance in this endeavor, the nature of the disease will play right into our hands. Your task is to support their denial and let the disease take its course.

The educated and employed churchgoers are one of our tastier targets because not only are they subject to denial like anyone else, but they are particularly vulnerable to the flaw of comparison. The combination of these two temptations is almost unbeatable and I urge you to act accordingly. This type of person always has visible others apparently much worse off—the street winos, derelicts, those who lose their jobs repeatedly or lose their families due to alcohol. It should be a relatively easy task to nurture their denial of their own disease. Feed their thoughts that they are well-respected in their communities, in their churches and businesses. Whenever they are inclined to think that they have a problem, insinuate into their thoughts the view of the alcoholic as one who has lost everything. Already eager to avoid the truth, they will then readily convince themselves that they must be overreacting. You might even toy with their efforts to cut down on their drinking for awhile; let them have small successes. This will delay the inevitable and let us enjoy the fare all the more. Humans caught in denial can fool themselves for years, and I need not remind you that it is always our job to abort the truth!

You will recall from your preparation that it is often more to our advantage with some clients to avoid any intense experiences which might precipitate a journey into recovery. It is sometimes better to support some of them (carefully selected for maximum long-term destruction) in abstinence for awhile. Most of them do not really understand that the disease itself progresses. When they resume their alcohol use, they will be caught completely off guard by the swiftness of their return to even heavier drinking than they knew before.

Encourage them to feel slightly superior to those who have had encounters with the law or have lost jobs. Let them feel a devilish confidence that they can "handle it." Let them keep just enough control that their drinking fails to cause enough trouble in their lives to lead to change. In the meantime, nurture their selfishness and self-seeking. Feed their fears and anxieties. Deform their instincts, basically good as given by the Enemy, for our designs. I have always found it particularly savory to watch the hardening of their hearts and souls as they do more and more to protect their drinking habits. They want to think that they are hurting no one. They still perform acceptably at work, still tuck their children in at night, still go to church regularly. In short, they will not consciously recognize the insidious and tasty narrowing of their measly lives as we bring them ever closer to our side. They will not recognize, with your help, the lack of truth or vitality that you have nurtured in their relationships. As long as their drinking involves no major crises, particularly those which might be public, they will be blind to the spiritual havoc they are contributing to those close to them. Whatever healthy resolutions they might make, let them be compromised so real change does not occur.

People who regularly pray or go to church always make a nice dessert for our consumption. These people often have the further delusion that they are close to God because they say words and sing songs of praise. (Even better when they are joined by their families, each member pretending the grand lie that all is well). It does not seem to matter to them much that the Son spoke out quite clearly about the necessity for doing His Father's will rather than just parroting words. Let them stay in inaction as long as possible. You will, of course, be enhancing our victories by eroding their relationships in a slow, simmering way. Every time we can help them make a hollow promise to the Creator to do something about their drinking, it is a gain for us. They still want to believe that they have the power to control their drinking. Block any realization of theirs that they are powerless and that only the Enemy has the power they crave. Actually, for many alcoholics it would be difficult to discern which they crave the more: alcohol or control.

Good rot with this type. I believe that you will find it particularly enjoyable.

Sincerely,
Screwtape

Letter 3

Dear Rotbranch,

You must constantly be open to new opportunities to lead mortals into darkness; one of the surest ways is through their human relationships. This century has seen an almost unbelievable distortion in what these mortals believe that relationships should produce: unfailing intimacy, constant understanding, an almost mystical oneness (with ample room for independence), an enduring feeling of love—the list is almost endless. Many of them fully expect these qualities, and the absence of any real pain along the way! Since their expectations are almost celestial and their realities quite earth-bound, it is no wonder that so many of them end up with far more unhappiness than they knew possible. If we had the capacity to laugh, this would indeed be laughable.

It is not that alcoholics or their loved ones are much different from others in this respect; rather, alcoholics are quite incapable of forming truly healthy relationships when they are in the grip of their addiction. As one of them once said, they don't make relationships, they take hostages. For all practical purposes, they stop growing about the time they start relying on alcohol to solve their problems. The disease stunts their emotional and spiritual growth; this gives you many avenues to forge foul failings in their relationships.

Any of these human love relationships can be counted on to produce pain along the way, but those who are relatively freer of addictions or compulsions can utilize the pain to produce healthy growth. This seems to be how the Creator operates as well. He'll prune here and there in order to produce the growth He wants, but oh, how they howl when they are cut! If you are afflicting them properly, those with the disease of alcoholism will be largely unable to utilize their pain for any growth-producing effects. They will learn nothing from their suffering and will keep repeating the same mistakes over and over. Let them find no enlightenment, nor wisdom, nor inspiration in their wontedness. Keep them in our darkness!

Marriages with an alcoholic will endure many hardships: if not economic, then emotional and spiritual. Wives, in particular, having been socialized to take care of their husbands, will endure years of unpredictability and pain while their husbands are drinking. One of your best ways to rack the women is to keep them in a constant mind of uncertainty, but you must blind them to the toll this is taking on their serenity. Since the husband's active alcoholism is only going to get worse without your help, all you need do is be inventive in adding to the misery. It is quite entertaining to watch the alcoholic make promise after promise and to see the spouse raise hope after hope, and then to see it all disintegrate in the face of the disease. Remember your instructions to block any inclination to surrender to the Enemy. The last thing we want in our hell is for the alcoholic to admit their own powerlessness over their drinking or for the spouse to admit their helplessness in changing their mate. You can do as much damage in relationships as you can within a given soul if you cleverly manipulate their frailties.

Since they have been emotionally and spiritually stunted, alcoholics will have the tendency to think of themselves, their own needs, wants and whims. Again, this is not all that different from the vast majority of the human race. What is different is that the active alcoholic is quite incapable of getting outside of self long enough to sustain a healthy relationship. As the disease progresses, more and more will have to be done to protect the addiction, which means that more and more will be unavailable for the other person or the relationship. No relationship can thrive if it is deprived of ongoing sustenance. Your task is to block, in the alcoholic, any genuine selflessness or giving; and to block in the spouse or children any genuine understanding or acceptance. In cases where the disease progresses rapidly, as it does for some of these humans, you can assist the quick disintegration of relationships. In humans where the disease itself progresses slowly, as is more often the case, you can enjoy long years of their agony. I myself always prefer the latter.

You will find, as you gain more experience with mortal marriage and family, that many of these creatures have enormous endurance for pain. That is fine for our purposes as long as no constructive use is made of the pain. Allow no learning, no insight to take place. While He may use pain for His own purposes, we must direct as much as we can to Our Father Below. I wish that we could take credit for the disease itself, but we cannot. We can take credit for using the disease to promote evil and, quite gratifyingly, loss to the Enemy. In human life most of their hopes and aspirations, their sorrows and joys, are experienced in relationships. That such relationships should be a magnet for more than they bargained for usually comes as a surprise to them, as if their relationships were somehow outside the flow of life—if you can imagine! What most do not know, unless we have done our job sloppily, is that relationships are also a magnet for *our* efforts. Humans have a saying, "two heads are better than one"; for our purposes, "two souls are better than one." Anytime you can help corrupt a soul and simultaneously promote chaos in a relationship, you have done your job well.

Sincerely,
Screwtape

Letter 4

Dear Rotbranch,

Your work with Matthew has been exceptional. It greatly pleases me that you have so well learned the lesson, "teach them to lie and make them a slave." Virtually all of these scabrous humans detest being lied to, yet how many of them are capable of leading truthful lives?

True, the Enemy does give them His grace to have compassion and spare others unnecessary hurt when the greater Good is served by shading a truth too bold for the bearing. Fortunately for us, most of their lies and deceptions are self-serving, designed only to cover their own gutlessness. Matthew is such a good example, and your work with him so exemplary, that I may use him as a case study in the next class. He has become so accustomed to deception in order to minimize his drinking problem that he scarcely recognizes the truth. Outright lies now come as easily to him as breathing. He does not even need to think ahead to plan out his lies in order to make them convincing. He received the usual childhood teachings about truth, but since he so often saw half-truths and deceptions while growing up, his commitment to be honest was never more than half-developed. All he now has to do, thanks to you, is to spend a split second thinking of self-protection and the lie just comes spewing from his lips. It does not even matter that much if the truth would be just as easy.

Thanks to your masterful handling, he is almost totally unaware of the energy his deceptions and distortions are costing him. Although he recognizes that he is tired much of the time, he simply doesn't see that much of his fatigue is trying to live more than one life. He knows that he has to remember what he has said so as not to entrap himself with his previous deceptions. If he gave it half a thought (your job to continue blocking) he would realize that much of his listlessness and weariness is due to the conscious fears that his deceptions will be discovered. He fears that he himself will become exposed. Fine. This is as it should be. Help him weave his tangled web and then he will invest so much energy in protecting the web from intrusion that he'll have little energy or devotion left for anything truly positive in his life.

Best of all, and this truly brings me glee, is that you have helped him convince himself that he is a noble person for covering up the truth! Remind him that he is doing good, is good, by sparing others the truth. In some people this might be so, but in him it is such a blatant and self-serving falsehood that I am astonished that he does not see right through it! Blindness, blindness! Wonderful blindness.

While I think that there is little likelihood in the near future that he will confront the dishonesty of his life and the way he is living, it is well to remember that God stands ever ready to help him back to His fold. Why He still loves these beings after all their broken promises to amend their lives, we will never know. But love them He does and you must not show any easing of your tenacity in helping Matthew to maintain his dishonesty. Should something happen to create a change of heart in him— perhaps a crisis event in which he admits his powerlessness over alcohol and begins recovery—or is somehow touched by how rotted his life has become, you must be ready to pounce.

If he should take steps toward honesty and integrity, and you are unable to continue nurturing his ever-present fears of being found out, then the best strategy is to lead him into an abrupt and explosive fit of honesty. In this event you would encourage him to disclose the worst wrongs he has committed to those who will be hurt the most. Let him hold nothing back. Blind him to compassion in the vomitous purging of his misdeeds. You may be tempted to think that we should prevent total and unreserved honesty since we work so diabolically to maintain its opposite. After you have had a few cases like this you will begin to see the benefit to us of the sudden and premature disclosure. At best, he will cause so much pain in those who love and trust him the most that he will drive them further away from him. Once he sees, really sees, the pain he has caused, then he will likely overreact to his own sinfulness and become more isolated than ever. With a bit of prodding you can remind him how much easier it was when he was still drinking. He will then have even more reason to hate himself because he now has not only fully exposed himself, he has—he believes—ruined the lives of others.

Above all, keep him away from any wise counsel that would help him become more honest in a temperate and compassionate way. Like so many alcoholics, Matthew is a man of excesses, blacks and whites. Blind him to the middle road and you more readily guarantee our victory. His long years of drinking and dishonesty have produced both bodily and mental distortions. Having seen things almost solely through his own eyes for so long, he will have little sense of balance. It is probably best to keep him in the active drinking state as long as possible, but opportunities await us even if he should somehow decide to get off the bottle.

Sincerely,
Screwtape

tial for a woman's self-esteem when you can weave shame into the cloak of failure which many of them wear.

Recall from your training the chemical effects which alcohol induces into the mortal brain. You know as well as I do that, beyond small amounts, alcohol has a depressive effect. That is the nature of the drug and humans are reluctant to learn the truth of this. Fortunately for us, many of them will drink even more to try and produce the effect which they think they want—blissful enjoyment. They might as well wish for the rising sun to hold itself in a static position so they can enjoy it a few moments longer. Wishing changes nothing. They simply cannot continue to drink and stay in some static state of enjoyment. They are either going to get drunk or get sober!

Particularly in some people, already prone to depression by their brain chemistry, alcohol itself can further the effect of melancholy, meaninglessness and misery. What a wonderful combination! Mary has not made this connection yet and is inclined to drink to make herself feel better, just like all those with the disease. The fact that it ends up making her feel worse places her in an endless cycle of dispiritedness; this is exactly where we want her. It should be little effort for you to remind her that another drink would help her to feel better when she is already a little down. Since she has the disease, there is almost no way that she can limit herself to one drink. The first drink can be counted on to trigger the craving in her brain for more; you don't even have to work on this part. The disease will do it for you. Your only work is to lead her to acquiesce to the temptation of the first drink. Her brain chemistry will take over from there and lead her to consume more than she intended or wanted.

The foul ease of this is twofold, either of which would be delectable but together make a feast for us. First, alcohol itself will chemically exaggerate her depressive feelings since her brain is predisposed to produce this reaction. Only the Creator knows why some of these humans have this exaggerated response and others do not. We do not need to know the why of it; it is sufficient for our purposes to exploit it for their misery and despair. Second, since she will certainly surpass her intended drinking amount (count on it) she will feel that she has no will power and is, consequently, a bad person. She still thinks of her dependence on alcohol as a moral weakness; if you encourage this perception, you can deepen her depression. This suits our purposes well.

The pièce-de-résistance for this particular course is when you implant the suggestion that perhaps she should switch to a different kind of drink. Lead her to believe that this will enable her to get her drinking under control. Humans with the disease will do almost anything to avoid facing the truth that they simply cannot drink in normal amounts. I notice that bourbon has been her drug of choice. I would recommend vodka as a substitute for her. You can lead her to believe that this is better for her because it is a clear alcohol. I know that you will find that hard to believe, but she will want to believe anything at this point. Some of our greatest amusements are found in watching them writhe their way through different drinking plans trying to find a miraculous solution which allows them to continue drinking.

If she switches to vodka, her family may not notice for awhile how strong she is making her drinks and slow down their nagging of her to stop. That is fine for us. With her distorted thinking, she will interpret their reaction as a positive sign, since she is looking for hope (not Hope) wherever she can find it. If you are properly deceptive, she will fail to notice that she is drinking more and more. In truth, she will know this, but will not admit it to herself. The alcohol will continue to have its depressive effect and you have thus advanced the desired effect: a feeling of gray, lifeless hopelessness. Mary will feel less and less of anything, except of course her own growing detachment from anything that has really mattered to her.

If this is so easy that it begins to bore you, you may want to toy with her angers. She tries so hard to be nice to everybody that she is completely out of touch with her angry side. Most humans do not realize that many of their depressions are a result of turning their angers inward upon themselves. Our success with this ploy, especially for women, has staggered our planners. Unfortunately for us, most of the human cultures give men so much license to express their angers that the depression stratagem seldom works well with them. No matter. Where we get women with self-destruction we get men with the destruction of others.

If you cannot abort Mary's peace by blinding her to her disease, her chemical tendency toward depression and her buried angers, you do not deserve another soul. You know that we are watching you—always.

Sincerely,
Screwtape

Letter 6

Dear Rotbranch,

Your last letter was totally unacceptable! How dare you think of accusing me of an omission in your training! Do not whine to me about your own inadequacies, look to yourself! Perhaps you have been working with humans too long—you're starting to make excuses. I know that we did not give you specific instructions for dealing with alcoholism in young people. Do we have to tell you everything? Your instructors and I assumed, evidently incorrectly, that you would be able to apply the diabolical strategies wherever the situation might fit. Of course they fit with young people! You have particularly good openings with those at younger ages.

The disease (recall your instructions, you fool!) progresses at different rates in humans; only He knows why. You don't need to know why. You just need to be alert to new avenues for us. In some humans, the signs and symptoms of alcoholism will not become very evident until they are middle-age, in others, much earlier. You cannot induce the disease in anyone; all you can do is distort the effects for our purposes. Teenagers and young adults are no exception—how could you not know this? Many young people today start drinking when they are still in

19

their early teens, usually disguised from their parents, of course. Most of them, like most adults, do not have the disease, but many of them do. Your task is simple: as rapidly as possible identify the ones who are susceptible and begin your destruction. Some alcoholics, later in life, will admit that they knew they had a problem while they were still in their teens; they knew, in a rather unusual insight for mortals, that they enjoyed drinking and were drawn to it much more than their peers. As I have pointed out elsewhere, we have been able to inculcate in some cultures a pride in excessive drinking. Young people in these cultures, following the adult lead, will quickly learn to take the same pride in being able to consume large amounts of alcohol. If you work with any degree of cunning, this pride will remain despite the fact that it often makes them feel awful, undermines their education, and confuses them very much. What more could we want?

You have special opportunities with young people, those in their teens and twenties; it makes little difference if you are dealing with boys or girls. They are even more ignorant of the facts of the disease than are adults and are especially unlikely to confront the truth. Whereas you can often lead an older adult to a point where jobs, homes and marriages are threatened or lost, you do not have quite the same leverage with the younger crowd. Since they have not yet accumulated much they have less to lose, except their spirit of course! So many mortals are ignorant that parents, even when they do find out about their child's drinking, are loathe to accept that one of theirs has alcoholism. As if this were some black mark against their souls! There are many families where young people, finally trying to confront the truth of their addiction, disclose to their parents what they believe to be the truth and their parents try to talk them out of the belief! Encourage this blindness. Naturally, young people do not want to believe that it is true either, so many of them will grasp at their parents' denial to reinforce their own. Oh, how wonderful this is! It takes a special courage for a person in their teens or twenties to confront their alcoholism; your job is to discourage and make their families as nonsupportive as possible. Where you cannot instill disbelief in the parents, instead promote a harsh judgmentalism and disapproval. Young people will already feel a bit shaky because they know they are different; prod their parents to make them feel badly about themselves and you will have advanced our cause greatly. Even if you cannot poison the parent-child relationship, you can gnaw at the young person's self-esteem.

Your task will be more difficult in this respect when one of the parents or immediate kin is an acknowledged alcoholic. Since the thread of alcoholism sometimes runs in families, a young person may have someone biologically close who has the same disease. However, it is easier for us if the parents do not have the disease; that way you can feed their critical and reproachful reactions. One or more of the grandparents may have been so afflicted. Many mortals still do not understand that genetic predispositions can easily skip a generation before reappearing, despite over a hundred years of scientific evidence. You would think that they would finally catch on; but ignorance is bliss and mortals would almost always rather lead blissful lives than truthful ones.

If one of the parents does have alcoholism, you will have to work more viciously with the entire family. It is a great advantage to us if the alcoholic parent is living in denial of their own disease. It is then virtually impossible for them to accept their child's alcoholism and increasing deterioration without facing themselves at the same time. With some careful evil you can encourage the mutual denial of both parent and child. Why blind just one if you can rot two souls with the same effort?

If an alcoholic parent is in recovery, there is still opportunity for you to afflict the young person. Lead the parent to be self-righteous and critical, or torment the parent with the thought that it is their fault that the child has the disease. Goad the parents to think of "saving" their child as their responsibility. If you can lead the parents into this trap they will undoubtedly come to view their own worth in terms of their success or failure in "saving" the child. Hah!

This strategy will not work very well for those who are truly living their recovery programs: they will have learned that they cannot change another, no matter how great the desire. They will have learned that all they can do is make the effort to help; the result is up to the cursed Creator. They will have learned that their son's or daughter's disease is beyond their control. In short, the disgusting vermin will turn this, too, over to Him.

When you cannot get the parent to take your bait, then redouble your effort with the young person. It is especially difficult for young people to recognize and accept the fact that they are alcoholics; until they do, there is little chance of change and healthy growth. Keep them blind. Remind them over and over that they have a right to be "normal," that they don't deserve the disease and don't want it. Lead them to magnify all that they will have to give up if they have to stop drinking, and abort any thoughts or realization that they will find far more happiness in recovery than they have in the drug.

Like adults, it is often to our advantage to protect the teen or young adult from any catastrophic experiences with alcohol lest they have no choice but to face the truth of their disease. Instead, let them settle into a slow and destructive deterioration which you should be able to prolong for many years. I feel a special fullness when we can so torment young people's lives, because I suspect it makes Him weep.

Sincerely,
Screwtape

Letter 7

Dear Rotbranch,

Accounts of your work with Elizabeth from some of your colleagues are most encouraging. They say that you have been quite successful thus far in blinding her family and friends to her obvious alcoholism. True, she has become very suspicious about her dependence on alcohol and is harboring worries that she has the disease.

I could almost feel sorry for her, except that it is not in my capacity; women endure far more stress than men, but become active alcoholics less often. When they do, men and women alike (isn't the hypocrisy wonderful!) judge the woman with alcohol problems far more severely than they do the man. Small wonder that the disease remains far more secretive for women.

Early public visibility of alcohol problems in women is not usually to our advantage. You were quite correct to discourage her from drinking very often in public places where her habits might be noticed. Far better to lead her to drink at home, and alone, when the husband and children are gone. So far you have accomplished this admirably. In time, it will help if you can nurture her growing guilt about her drinking, but do not overdo it. We want her to feel guilty enough to be wretched but not so

much that she makes any kind of decision to stop. Women especially can remain closet alcoholics for a very long time. By-
and-large, they have not developed any of the foolhardy beliefs
that many men have about drinking; for instance, men who believe that it is some sign of masculinity to be able to consume
enormous quantities of alcohol without passing out. Even if their
physical self-destruction in the process were not abhorrent to the
Enemy, certainly the false pride that they take in such action
would be. Your predecessors worked many years to help implant
that irony among men and we have reaped our just desserts.
The same tactic never progressed very far among women, so we
have had to develop other strategies. Since they are more likely
to be closet drinkers, we can bring to women somewhat different
kinds of self-destruction than men. I know that you appreciate
as much as I do a lingering meal of hopelessness, rather than a
quick snack of despair.

Don't be deceived by her husband's loving support if he dis-
covers the extent of her alcohol dependence. Most men have very
little tolerance for their wives' drinking problems and will often
give up and leave in a very short time. It is diabolically ironic
that these same husbands would feel morally and self-righ-
teously entitled to unconditional love and support if the situation
were reversed. Put many of them in a position where they actually have to support and nurture for awhile, and think of someone else's need other than their own, and they will quickly crum-
ble. It amazes even me that they would provide such support to
a good buddy, but their wives are in a special category; the men
act as if it is a personal affront to them that their wives have a
problem with alcohol. Sometimes we are successful beyond my
wildest dreams.

It is not particularly to our advantage one way or the other
if husbands stay or leave. In either case, your female clients will
feel endless guilt, as if they had asked for the disease or chosen
the suffering. Hah! It should be relatively easy for you to lead a
wife to become mired in shame, and the resulting inertia is
greatly to our benefit. If the husband leaves, the wife can be
persuaded to take full responsibility for his actions, with the con-

sequent suffering on her part. It doesn't matter much that he had his own problems that she had to deal with; likely as not, his were far more the result of choice than hers.

If he stays, do not think for a moment that we have lost. Sometimes we have greater opportunities in this situation. You can lead him to protracted resentment, judgment and criticism by preventing him from truly understanding that his wife has a disease. If he should show signs of developing such an understanding, undermine the thought by focusing his attention on himself. Since alcohol is not a problem for him, he can take it or leave it. Encourage him to make the same conclusion about his wife and you will have succeeded in blocking any real understanding, because he is interpreting life through only his own experience. It helps us if the husband has a hard time getting out of himself long enough to be empathic.

You will find an occasional husband quite different from most, one who understands and accepts the reality of his wife's illness and who is comfortable being loving and supportive. Do not waste your time trying to plant seeds of resentment with such men; they will not take root and you will have missed other opportunities. Your best avenue in such a situation is to nurture his pride through his self-congratulatory view of himself. Since he is human, he is bound to follow you into this trap. Your task is to see to it that these sentiments grow. Encourage him to see himself as the answer to her problems and prayers: *he* will see her through this, *his* love will become the vehicle for her recovery! In short, even if she turns toward God we will have ensnared the husband into forgetting Who it is that is doing the healing.

Humans love to take credit where none is due and deny blame when it should be embraced; men, especially, are masters at this.

Sincerely,
Screwtape

Letter 8

Dear Rotbranch,

It appears that Mark is going to stick to his resolution to not drink and I would not further torment him with the drinking temptation right now. You might even want to ease the pain of withdrawal and lead him to congratulate himself on what a noble person he is for making this heroic sacrifice. Let him feel pride in his self-proclaimed virtuousness. Encourage him to believe that he has done enough, that he's got it made. Since he has the disease, he is satisfied with the sacrifice it is for him to forego this pleasure, but he is blind to all aspects of alcoholism except the direct and visible consequences of drinking. Keep him that way.

With some careful preparation on your part, you should be able to preserve him for years as what these humans call a "dry drunk." At some point we will probably want to induce his active drinking again, but we can accomplish more damage now by encouraging him in his self-deception. He wants to think that recovery programs are only to help people stop drinking. Mark conveniently misses the whole point that such programs help people recover their lives! Abstinence without recovery we can use. Abstinence through recovery, and the programs that promote this are our bane: curse them forever! Inflate his pride that he has quit drinking on his own and blind him to the character defects which you can aggravate in the decay of his life. It should not be too difficult to confuse Mark with self-deception. Since he really is ignorant of the impact of alcoholism on his thinking and feeling, try to keep him in the dark as long as possible. Should he have any thoughts of joining a recovery program, block these with appeals to his pride.

Your best avenue with Mark is to nurture his selfishness, anger and judgmentalism. All humans are, by nature, self-centered. The Enemy seems to have created them so that their life journeys Home toward Him would require the sacrifice of self as part of the transformational process. He gives them life, and then wants them to turn it over to Him; the fact that so many of them do so proves that we have not been doing our work well enough. Fortunately, there are multiple paths available to us to impede and destroy the transformational process. It is not that Mark is that much more selfish than anyone else, rather, he is blind to himself. Thinking that he is being selfless, he still manages to think of everything in terms of how it is going to affect him. He tries to control other people, manipulate them (although he almost never sees this) to his way and his thinking. Since he is not a blatantly bad person in the conventions of the day, it is easy for him to deceive himself into thinking that what he believes is right is truth. Nurture this tendency. Especially now that he has given up drinking, you should have fertile opportunity to enlarge his self-deception. He wants to feel good about himself, wants to believe that he is a better soul than most. This one achievement of abstinence can be used as fodder to enhance his self-perception that he is a very, very good person, and is doing enough.

Since he is inclined to interpret everything from his own needs and wants, you will find much satisfaction in aggravating his judgments of others. His wife and children have their own faults and blind spots, of course, but they are not nearly as bad as he imagines them to be. Lead him to magnify the errors of their ways. Breed his obsession to take everything personally.

Since he likes a very tidy home and not all of his family are like this, keep him in a state of turmoil with what he sees as their messiness. Remind him that if only they loved him more, they would do as he wanted. Since almost no humans have the same standards of exactly how the home should be, this route for disrupting harmony is virtually always open to you. Let him feel in his gut that he has a right to have things the way he wants. Above all, keep from his mind any thought that each of the others in the family has the same rights that he does. Blind him to any effort to see things through their eyes.

If you can induce a sense of entitlement and judgment, he will remain at a slow boil most of his waking hours. The delicacy of this is that, with careful work on your part, he will never seriously question why he is angry so much of the time! He knows he is angry because he wakes up that way, moves through the day in this state of mind, prays that way and goes to sleep that way. Now that he no longer has his alcohol to use as a crutch, he is even angrier than he used to be. Keep his anger focused on other people.

In some families, rage-aholics will do even more damage than alcoholics, but with Mark you had best temper most of his temptations to rage. You might be inclined to dispute me on this but I am right. If he flies into a rage too often, he will begin to suspect that something is wrong with him, perhaps get suspicious that you are at work fueling his hostility. He might even receive an insight and be able to name his sin in this. As it now stands, he is often proud of himself for not having a rage more often than he does, and I congratulate you on bloating his pride.

You have effectively blinded him to any genuine acceptance of other people as they are. The best course with him is to lead him to keep most of his anger inside, focused on the failings of those closest to him. This will inevitably poison the home relationships and anytime we can accomplish the destruction of love, Our Father Below rejoices. Since Mark is angry most of the time, serenity is beyond his grasp; indeed, right now, he cannot even imagine it. I encourage you to remember the malediction I gave at your graduation. He will not know that, although he has stopped drinking, he has made no recovery from the effects of alcoholism on his thinking and feelings.

Should you want a nice dessert sometime, intrude yourself into his evening prayers. Regardless of the words he uses, let the prayer of his heart to the Enemy—his real prayer—be to change his family members. Blind him to the possibility that he might pray instead for acceptance. The grace of acceptance would solve most of his problems and put him squarely into the Creator's heart. We must prevent that at all costs.

Mark is not in any recovery program, but believes himself to be "recovered." Hah! Still, he might start feeling a bit guilty that he is not learning more about his disease. He prides himself on his intellectual approach to things, and likes to have everything figured out in terms that he can understand. This has worked well for us in the past and we can continue to use it. If he should pick up a book on the subject and run any risk of being enlightened, divert his understanding so that everything stays in his head. Let nothing of value settle into his heart where insight might take root and grow into true recovery and redemption.

Sincerely,
Screwtape

Letter 9

Dear Rotbranch,

Congratulations, my fiendish fellow! We can use your handling of Luke's family in our next class of devil novices. You have gone beyond your training to new depths of cunning. It was diabolical of you (I'd like to think that you have imitated me) to twist the early stages of his recovery to expose other problems of the family. The mental and spiritual turmoil which has ensued has been quite savory and I know that you are enjoying it as much as am I.

How very simple it had been for Luke's wife and children to blame all their unhappiness on his drinking. It is real enough that the effects of his disease have brought much pain into their lives, only some of which he will ever truly realize. He simply will not remember—nor understand when he does remember— the many times when his children were too embarrassed or apprehensive to invite their school chums over for a visit. He'll never know the pain of isolation this brought to them in their formative years. Nor will he understand at any depth the shame his wife felt with his behavior. Isn't it wonderfully foul how we have managed to get many of these humans to feel shame because of the behavior of a loved one? It is as if they think, by virtue of their love or family connections, that they are responsible for the choices made by another. We have gotten more than our temptation's worth out of mortal shame. If we had a few more emotions like that at our disposable we could easily rule the world; their God would not stand a chance.

Since Luke has stopped drinking, at least for now, the entire family has been set up to believe that life would be smooth once again. A lesser devil might have been content at this point, but you have hounded the family with gratifying insidiousness. Once Luke owned up to his responsibility for family problems, the whole family breathed a sigh of relief. Prematurely, you devil! (Here, Screwtape emits a rare sound. Humans might call it something like a laugh, but with a sinister enjoyment that foreshadows great potential for destruction—evil with eyes wide open in anticipation). Little did they realize what you had prepared!

Deprived of the focal point they have had for so many years, they now have more time and mental energy to realize something about themselves: they've got their own problems! Their own! Mara has finally realized that it was she alone who made the decision to not take the promotion at work, allegedly for family, but more truly because of her own fears. James is quite bewildered about sex, as is true of many teenage boys. Thanks to us, it is almost impossible for him to know what might be healthy sexual values and behavior. Feel free to torment him with impossible fantasies which will grind against the values he does have. Luke's daughter has slowly begun to realize that she will never be the glamorous woman with flawless figure that she so wants to be. I, of all devils, can brag for helping to create much of the current scene, where both women and men idolize the flawless female body, and anything less is hardly worth noticing. The potential of nursing his daughter's resentment over her physical normalcy should reap great rewards for you. I remember how we vexed Moses' people with golden calves. That was nothing compared to the idolatry of superficial beauty as *the* standard for women with which we have cultivated and corrupted this century. Not even we had any idea how much we could get girls and women to dislike themselves with this effort.

Now that Luke is not the apparent magnet for all the problems and pain, the others are freer to feel their own. You have done quite well in fermenting personal discontent, and all is grist for our meal. Feelings and emotions within the family have reached a new level of rawness. The family is thinking, secretly, that it was almost easier when Luke was actively drinking—at least then they had an idea of what was going on. These feelings are all natural, of course, but provide us great opportunities for fermenting agony. One of the human family once said, in a moment of rare insight, that it is easier for them to walk the familiar paths of hell than the unknown paths of heaven. Thanks be to Our Father Below!

You have cultivated their bewilderment and dissatisfaction quite well. Humans want everything to be better all at once. They want to ignore the fact that the Creator does not want them to be overly content for too long in the life of the world, lest they forget where real happiness lies. As far as you've gone, all is well. Their personal and family turmoil suits our purposes.

You must be on guard and not let the turmoil become too intense if there is any chance that such intensity would goad them into getting help for the whole family. Right now, they are still trapped in the myopic thought that most of the family problems have been due to Luke's drinking, and that recovery is only his business. They have been so blinded to their own problems by the tyranny of Luke's drinking that they don't recognize how their own growth has been stunted. Keep his wife and children away from any support groups which might provide either help or spiritual insights; best to keep them blind as long as possible. Even though they are making inroads toward accepting others, since Luke cannot help but spout his new philosophy, it is crucial to our purposes that they not accept themselves as they are. Try to keep them all in a state of confused but unexpressed agitation: his wife about what she might have had in a career, his son about his own body, and his daughter about the cruelty of fate that being simply pretty is not enough. With some finesse on your part, you should be able to disrupt any efforts they might make in accepting themselves, even if they do accept others. Many will never realize the paradox.

They may see what is happening in time, but as long as we can disrupt their peace of mind, or peace in any form, we have impeded their spiritual growth. Moreover, now that their hopes have soared for a new family, let them grieve over the death of their dreams without ever realizing that what they wanted was only everything.

I will remind you that neophyte devils sometimes make the mistake of overkill, believing that the best way to gain victory is to seek an absolute rejection of the good of the Enemy. That this sometimes succeeds but often backfires is well established. Archevil, of which I consider myself a master, is slower, more patient and infinitely more tasty. Should you aspire to lower things, I encourage you to consider this strategy. Is it not more enjoyable to us to watch the slow dissolution of the spirit—struggling, gasping, almost making it—than to too quickly enjoy an easy victory? I am confident that you will make the most destructive choice.

Sincerely,
Screwtape

Letter 10

Dear Rotbranch,

You have badly bungled your work with Anna. There is no excuse for you to have permitted her to get into so much pain. Your preparation and tutelage were very precise on this point, and I can only surmise that you are either incredibly stupid or stupidly careless.

Do you not remember—although it was drilled into each of you over and over—that mortals can bear much, but that when the pain becomes too great they change? Our task has always been to keep them just short of that point at which they surrender and admit their own powerlessness. This point too often brings a sincere motivation to do something (with the help of the Enemy, who is all too ready to assist their slimy souls). You must remember all the years spent in creating just the right amount of helplessness and anguish over drinking that they could never be truly happy nor well connected with the Creator. We tutored you for years in devilish instruction regarding slow agony as the preferred path. Years and much, much experience undergird the wisdom of sheltering them from too much pain. Have you forgotten how we even manage to lead them to think that it is always their Creator who has spared them more than they can handle, and keep them on the path of thinking they can manage alcohol?

It is clear that your instructions were precise, which makes your failure with her all the more despicable. You were entrusted with a soul well on the way to a protracted agony over her inability to stop drinking. She never got so drunk nor so obnoxious, never got into so much trouble—even with her family—that her plight was evident. Her family covered up well enough for her, not knowing how they were playing into our hands by their excuses and tenderness and constant insufferable helpfulness. No matter. The fault is yours entirely; theirs I can blame on ignorance, but your mistake was inexcusable.

However could you have led her to drink right before picking up her daughter from day-care and then missing that stop sign? Were you out of your mind to have permitted that accident? Don't even think of protesting that it was just a small accident with no real harm done.

No physical harm was done; the real harm is done! Harm to us, you fool, great harm to our purpose! Anna has become so filled with painful regrets that there is now virtually no way of stopping her from getting help. You know as well as I that she has made countless promises to her family, even more to herself, and many to God that she would soon quit drinking. But human promises about addictions usually have no strength until they are fortified by great pain. What should have been easy prey for you, and food for our consumption, is now made exceedingly difficult. I frankly see little chance at the moment of reclaiming her anguish for our own purposes. What she could not accomplish by herself now has a good chance of being achieved through the intervention of the Infinite Good and all those fools who believe in recovery. These things obey pain! It is always your task to lead them into pain and a rejection of the Enemy, but not so much pain that they are forced to finally face themselves and make some changes in their lives.

You may be thinking that the worst of this is that her family and friends now have a clearer idea of her dependence on alcohol and will pressure her to give it up. Not so. In this case, her family and friends can help us or harm us little. The real loss is that she is, finally, facing the truth about her addiction. True, she has lived in fear for many years that she would be "found out," that those who love her would come to realize that this was more than an occasional problem with her. This fear served our purposes quite well because it disrupted her life and weakened her soul. Her writhing within herself was quite the dish for us. For years she has been secretly drinking before and after her more open drinking with family and friends. They were often puzzled by how much she seemed to react to just one or two drinks, not knowing that she had already consumed quite a bit before their get-togethers. They had even laughed at her inability to "hold it" as well as they could. She has carried the secret as best she could, first easily and later with ever more weariness.

Since Anna is basically a good mother, she has had all the normal mother fears that she wasn't doing enough for her children, was letting them down somehow, was really failing them in a crucial way. We could have prolonged her agonies over her children and caused cancerous rot for years, had it not been for this accident. Now she knows that she must change, and she is of the type that her resolve will not be easily shaken.

I should not need to remind you of this but you have bungled so badly that I wish to take no chances. As Anna contemplates recovery, let her imagine an endless succession of days without alcohol. Remind her of her broken promises to herself from the past. Nurture her fears that she really cannot handle "the future." Do whatever you must to block any thoughts of living one day at a time. Mortals who have entered recovery programs and have learned this lesson are much more difficult to seduce away from the Enemy. He wants them to live in the present; we want them to be torn between their guilts of the past and their fears of the future. As it is now, too many of them are discovering that living one day at a time is a surer path to follow for their own happiness and spiritual benefit.

One of theirs, G. K. Chesterton, once said that "angels can fly because they take themselves lightly." Such thinking is poison for our purposes. Your task with Anna, and all others, is to make their hearts and souls heavy with anxieties. Lead them to live and think and feel anything but the present.

Sincerely,
Screwtape

Letter 11

Dear Rotbranch,

Your whimpering to me about John was disdainful. Do you really think that he is beyond our reach just because he has admitted his powerlessness over alcohol? Do you really anticipate an automatic conversion to the Enemy's path? Believe that there are no more opportunities for us? If so, you are far less evil than I had believed and, perhaps, unfit for the work you have been assigned.

This is a setback, you fool, only a setback! Certainly you are up to the challenge! Did we teach you to cringe at such obstacles? Of course not! True, all it takes sometimes is for these humans to make a turn to the Enemy; they don't even have to go far before He comes rushing right in to carry their wounded souls. Remember the Son's story where the old father rushed to greet his derelict son "while he was still a long way off"? Nonetheless, do not be discouraged. As yet, John is still well within our influence.

He will be feeling a mixture of both exhilaration and fear: exhilaration that maybe, just maybe, his living nightmare of alcohol addiction may be over; and fear for the same reason, that his drinking might be over. Right now there is no way that he can imagine a life without alcohol. Your best strategy is to gnaw at him with the idea that he will never be able to drink again. Get him to fantasize about his entire future—without drinking. Let him imagine those quiet peaceful moments where a drink is absolutely pleasant, those stressful moments where a drink is absolutely necessary, those celebrations where drinking is part of the rituals. Encourage him to think far into the future, and feel helpless at his inability to figure it all out, his blindness to know how it will be. Regardless of how much pain alcohol has brought into his life, the prospect of getting by without his best friend will fill him with dread. Encourage this.

John is really at a pivotal point right now. Even if he gets into a recovery program, temporarily emboldened by the exhilaration of hope, all is not lost. If you properly foment his tendency to dread the future without alcohol, you can eventually recapture his active addiction. John's momentum for change comes from the cursed Creator, the damnable hope which He seems to plant in human souls. In this case it is best for you not to combat his momentum immediately. Within a short time the "pink cloud" of relief which now envelops him will be dissipated. In John's case, I believe that it is best to cast doubt and fear into his thinking. Since he has never been able to quit drinking for long before, nag him to think that he is, after all, just fooling himself. Remind him that *he* has failed before.

Above all, blind him to the realization that the Enemy can save him. Those fetid fools in recovery programs like AA have a shorthand way of remembering the first three steps of change: "I can't . . . He can . . . I think I'll let Him!" You *must* block this surrender in John. Keep him focused on himself, mired within *his* sense of powerlessness and hopelessness. If his mind should drift to thoughts of God, and you are unable to abort such an atrocity, try to get him to perceive the Enemy through his own eyes. Lead him to anthropomorphize God as a critical, judging, punitive deity. We know how far from Truth this is; but our man, gripped by his own sense of futility, will see everything as bleak. Let him reap the picture we have sown for centuries. Let him believe that He might save others, but not him, that he is not deserving. Lead him to think of himself as so thoroughly despicable as to be beyond help. Let him think of Him as a God of justice rather than mercy. Once his mind dwells on his sense of justice, within his own judgmental framework, there is little chance he will escape our trap.

At one time, John was helped by small amounts of alcohol. It helped him to be what he desperately wanted to be—more outgoing, relaxed, congenial, even empathic. He liked himself that way, wanted to be just like that. If he did not have the disease, then the helpful aspect might have remained. With the disease, alcohol has inevitably become a powerful and quite unmanageable part of his life. He will want, with your prodding, of course, to avert any need to quit drinking entirely. Your previous letters to me concerning him indicate that he has already tried dozens of different solutions: drinking only in the evenings, drinking only beer, trying to limit himself to a certain amount each day, drinking only as much as others are drinking. Of course, none of this has worked long for him and his sense of futility has only grown. Let him imagine that he will find some way to get his drinking under control, if only he can find the right balance. He simply does not realize yet (another reason to keep him away from recovery programs) that the disease has distorted his thinking, does not want to realize that he simply cannot drink and lead a healthy life. Should he have dawning thoughts that he might have to quit entirely, lead him to glamorize the past and conveniently suppress the great pain alcohol has brought into his life. Since he cannot imagine ever being truly able to quit drinking, and believes that the result—instead of just the effort—is up to him, he will be caught in a paradox of despair. He knows, deep down, that *he* cannot quit and also that *he* cannot go on. If you successfully divert any thoughts of recovery programs or of the Creator's help, you can keep him in a state of inner despair for a good long while. Humans have been brainwashed to believe that they can do anything if only they "put their mind to it." The absurd folly of this belief should have become evident to them long ago. Our success in this ploy has surpassed our highest infernal hopes.

One caution: assume that the Enemy is ever-present, ready at the slightest flicker of thought in John's mind to pick him up and carry him. At this stage, you must block such thinking. Remind him that God would not be bothered with his puny life.

Sincerely,
Screwtape

Letter 12

Dear Rotbranch,

There is no question but that you will have to proceed carefully with Joseph. We both foresaw, but could not prevent, the
genesis of his recovery. I do not blame you, for a change, for the
loss of his active addiction. Who knows why the Enemy provided
so much support to him during his last crisis? Nor do we know
why, having so long been blinded, he finally saw his addiction
for what it was. It is as if our veil was simply removed from his
eyes and the years of denial and self-deception were obliterated.
It infuriates and amazes me that His grace can undo so much of
our work so quickly. It is to your credit that you offered no sim-
pering excuses; since I know that you lie, I never fully believe
you. If I thought you had committed error with Joseph, you
would know my wrath. As it is, I can see no fault on your part;
we have simply been out-maneuvered on this one.

Very soon, he will reach a place in recovery where he is encouraged to turn his will and life over to the care of God. I suspect
that that will be your next major opportunity to interfere with this
cursed process and lure him back in our direction. Be prepared.

Everything you have told me about this mortal leads me to
believe that he is one of the thinking types who wants to have

everything figured out. The type of man who, despite great evidence to the contrary, still believes that he needs to understand something before he can proceed. Encourage him in this line of thought. Let him obsess about the process, trying to figure out exactly what it will mean to make a decision to turn his life over to a Higher Power. Let him project his own worst case scenarios: a complete loss of self, a sense of nothingness, an image of non-being. We know how ludicrous such projections are but, with careful management, you can maintain him in this state for months, perhaps longer. Many of those who have begun recovery never get through this step, and this failure is always a major victory for us.

It will be easier for you to win if you can minimize his talking with people who are further along in recovery than is he. Let him keep his thoughts to himself as much as possible and, again, overly rely on himself to figure things out. It is an amazement to me that so many of these mortals who really cannot understand the simplest of things that are right in front of their faces would presume to think that they should be able to understand the process of healing. This is not a complaint, of course; their ego needs to "understand" work greatly to our advantage. It is your task to perpetuate Joseph in this state of mind as long as possible. Blind him to the realization that all he need do is make a sincere and simple declaration of his desire to turn his life over to the Enemy. Keep him entrapped within himself and his obsession to understand everything that influences him.

You need not play your fear card any sooner than is necessary. There is no point in wasting the temptation to fear when lesser efforts will do. However, should you find him slipping from us and becoming increasingly ready to make a decision to turn his life over to the care of the Enemy, then it is time to engulf him in fears. Let him fear what will become of his life. Let him imagine that he will not have a life left; lead him to conclude that such a decision will imprison him in the unknown hands of the Enemy. Above all, blind him (whatever it takes) to the realization of Truth: that turning his life over to God will release him from the emotional and spiritual prison he has made for himself! This is imperative. Do not fail.

Humans are increasingly wary of our efforts to conjure up the image of the Enemy as harsh and punitive. One of our greatest potential losses in this century is their deep-seated belief (fear) that God is, after all, a judgmental and angry deity. We fed that image so well for so many centuries that its loss to us is almost incalculable. Our forecasters predict that, if present trends continue, the punitive image will be completely impotent for our designs within a few generations.

However, we still have ample time with Joseph. Much of what he learned in childhood portrayed the Enemy as an unintelligible mixture of vengeance and mercy, retribution and forgiveness. Joseph still carries within his heart this mixture, even though he consciously knows better. As he over-analyzes and thinks about what it means to turn his life over to the care of God, divert his attention from the idea of the *care* of God. Let him imagine making this decision for a very unpredictable deity. If you carefully advance this strategy, you can keep him immobilized for a long while. Joseph's fear of the unknown is no worse than any other human's. However, he is facing a major change in how he copes with day-to-day life without alcohol (and without being in control). He will be quite confused if he anticipates God as totally unpredictable—beast or benefactor. We know, ironically in a way that most humans cannot know while on earth, that their God's luminosity and goodness are beyond words, beyond their imagination. It is easier for them to imagine Him as a projection of themselves, kindly some of the time and quite malicious at other times. Feed this imagination.

Encourage Joseph to try to have everything figured out to his satisfaction before proceeding, remind him of his vengeful God image learned in childhood and nurture his confusion. Always remember to block any stray thought that he might pray for the will to have the will to turn his life over. The Enemy will accept almost any invitation to help, however fearfully requested.

Sincerely,
Screwtape

Letter 13

Dear Rotbranch,

It was good to get your last report and to learn of your continued advances with David. You have done a commendable job in keeping his mind and spirit trapped in regret over past misdeeds and effectively prevented him from living in the present where any healing might take place. I congratulate you on your success in this strategy.

As you were instructed and certainly have confirmed by now, those with the disease of alcoholism tend toward the extremes. They are given to think, even without our help, that they are either close to sainthood or the very incarnation of evil itself. Both extremes are equally misguided and either form of self-deception can work to our advantage. The first benefit, quite obvious to you, I am sure, is their consistent practice of denial of their real sins, the countless ways they turn down and turn away from the Enemy in everyday life as they go about their way and their will. Oh, yes, some may turn over their will to God in times of crisis (who would not look for rescue in a sinking rowboat?), but as soon as things start going a bit better, it is their will all the way. With very little prodding from you, they will once again want to be captains of their lives. As soon as life is on an even keel, they will forget that their best thinking has gotten them into their dilemmas and that they are not really qualified to pilot their own destinies. Keep it that way.

The second self-deception is also to our advantage; but here you have to be carefully diabolical and baffling, lest it be carried too far. It suits our purposes if David and others are led to wallow in their own regrets: after all, they have made their own choices, even if it was the best they could do at the time. If you keep him in a state of remorse and agitation, our work is easier because there is less possibility of gratitude. Most humans, with our help, never realize that He does a lot of pruning in their lives in order to get rid of false self and permit new growth. Their egos are rather large and anytime something is being cut away they feel the pain of the knife rather than the hope of new growth. They simply do not want to believe that the Creator knows what is best for them—and is working to that end. Part of your task is to entrap them within themselves, their egos, their pride; lead them to experience pain only as loss and blind them to resurrection. However, do not lead David too far along the path of being woefully convinced of his own hopelessness as a decent human being; the pain might become too great. Keep him just short of surrender.

Instead, let him experience small rays of esteem, but not enough to take away his self-diagnosis that he is basically a rotten person for all the things he has done. Lead him to start to feel that he is a decent chap, but then intrude upon his thought some recognition of past misdeeds. Since he is basically a decent fellow, self-recrimination and remorse come naturally to him and can be exploited for our benefit. Mortals are wont to forget that He who made the mountains and seas also made them of His own damnable Goodness. Nurture their forgetfulness that nothing which comes from the Enemy is bad.

As David's mind wanders through his regrets like a holiday through hell you can encourage his if-only thoughts. You know the routine: if only he had married the other woman instead, if only he had not had so many children, if only he had not gotten into the job he is in, if only he had not driven by the bar that night. As you know, the list is endless within most mortals. His recollection of the past is normal enough because if there is anything that man does not want to do, it is live in the present. Our job is to keep them regretting the past or worrying about the future—and thus relatively immune to healing. God's cleansing grace, so poisonous to us, flows only in moments of the present; it cannot be borrowed from the future nor saved from the past.

A note of caution. Keep David away from any of those cursed recovery programs, if possible. Those chaps are far too ready to confront his folly and teach him that it is normal enough to have regrets, but dangerous to make them his home. As he wants to believe, deep down, that his future is not already condemned to a painful reliving of his past, he would be ready to grasp at whatever hope they might offer. Places of recovery reek with hope and are destructive to us beyond words. He really meant what He said with the promise that "where two or three are gathered in my name, there I am found."

Humans cannot produce hope within themselves, it is always a gift from the Enemy. Unfortunately for us, hope can be contagious. I cannot overstress the importance of this enough. These recovering humans can do much damage to our cause. I have seen years of deviltry undone in the space of a moment as a mortal, opened by pain, is flooded by real hope flowing through those who have known the suffering. He is in their midst at those cursed meetings and you must be relentless in your afflictions. Above all, blind David and all mortals in your charge to any realization that His gift of healing is already taking place.

Sincerely,
Screwtape

Letter 14

Dear Rotbranch,

Your recent inquiry concerning humans and their relationship to the Enemy is both admirable and unforgivable. It is admirable that you want to learn more ways to enslave the mortals; it is unforgivable that you did not learn this while you were still in your classes. The lessons were most thoroughly covered and there can be no excuse for your failure to master them. Their despicable God wants His creatures to be happy, joyous and free. We want exactly the opposite, and it is to this end that all of your work must be directed.

The Christian path, indeed any spiritual path, is not an easy one for it requires the humans to set higher goals than their own instincts and impulses would dictate. Your strategy is to exacerbate their instincts and impulses. The spiritual path requires them to give up more and more of their egos in order to get more and more of Him. Since it is not in their basic nature to be selfless, we have ample opportunity to afflict their basic tendencies and lead them to Our Father Below. Our spiritless path is a simple one: do all we can to decay their connection with the Enemy.

Enslavement is a principle tool at your disposal. He wants them to be free, we want them trapped within themselves and hence less available to Him. While we are often unable to keep them enslaved to alcohol, in the form of either problem or disease, we can subjugate them with their tendency to guilt and shame. Of the two, guilt is probably less effective for our purposes. Oh, you would do well to nurture guilt wherever possible, keep them trapped in a sense of guilt for what they have done. The problem with their simple guilts is that they are relatively superficial in these humans; long lasting, but shallow. Guilt is only the feeling they have when they have done something wrong. Indeed, some of the time the Creator allows them to feel guilty because they have done something wrong, and their consciences, provided by Him, react to this much as stubbing a toe might remind them to watch where they are going. A little guilt may be healthy for them; it is to our advantage to entangle them in constant feelings of guilt so they become paralyzed into doing nothing.

It is far better for you to nurture shame. Shame is where we can really crucify them: torment their souls, corrupt their connection with the Enemy, and cripple their spiritual journey back to Him. Shame is at the core of their sense of being, a profound certainty that there is something inherently rotten or wrong with them. I trust that you are not too simple-minded to see the difference. When they feel guilty, they feel as if they have done something wrong; when they feel shame, they feel as if they themselves are wrong in creation. The fools can get past their guilt by making amends and improving their lives. While we want to block this, of course, it is far more advantageous for us to nurture their shame, entrap them in a conviction that they are innately flawed. Not only flawed, but uniquely flawed. Let them think of themselves as somehow a misshapen part of creation. Nurture this thought until it grows into an ever-present hatred of themselves.

One of the surest methods to lead a recovering alcoholic back to drink, and then deeper into despair, is the tried-and-true method of getting them to hate themselves. This works particularly well with women who, despite their greater proclivity for spirituality than men, nonetheless have been socialized by sick societies (thanks to your predecessors) to think poorly of themselves. Take a woman who has been sober for awhile, regardless of the progress she has made in recovery, and lead her slowly but certainly into a period of self-hate. Sustain this long enough and the results will be exactly what we desire. Even if she does not start her drinking addiction again, the simple process of self-doubt, self-loathing and lack of acceptance of herself as she is will create a barricade between her and the Enemy. He will never desert her, of course, but she does not feel this in such a state of mind and, as usual, will pay more attention to what she feels than what she knows. It is a rather delicious irony that the same woman who preaches and practices acceptance of others (almost regardless of provocation to her) will simultaneously despise herself for her flaws. A woman in this state of mind confirms that you have done your work well. If you keep reminding her of her own flaws and inflame this into self-hate, you will have her within our grasp.

So many of these humans have not learned that their God, for whatever perverted reasons He operates out of His goodness, loves them entirely. Has always loved them. Will always love them. He cannot desert them, only they can desert Him. They forget in the day-to-dayness of their lives what He asked of His Son, and forget that all is already forgiven. Strengthen their forgetfulness of their most basic of beliefs. Lead them to think that He might love everyone—except them.

Sincerely,
Screwtape

Letter 15

Dear Rotbranch,

Have you forgotten everything? You must be one of the most comatose devils ever to have graduated from my jurisdiction! One moment, just one moment that Simon turns his will over to God and you act as if all is lost. Writing me such a stupid, insipid letter! I should order you back right now to a lesser task that even you might be capable of: perhaps introducing people to lust. But you do seem to have potential talent and I would hate to waste you on something that any neophyte devil can do. Frankly, I could care less about you; but it would look bad on my record if my supposed protégé were to fail so badly, so quickly. I would be the fool to my colleagues. As you well know, we shrivel when someone ridicules us.

Think back: one of the first lessons you learned in primary deviltry was how self-oriented these humans really are. Do not think for a moment that your client will permanently maintain his resolve to turn his will over to the Enemy. No human alive has been able to do that, except that damnable Son of his. I know; I personally gave Him every opportunity to put His will first and He, curse Him forever, was faithful.

Fortunately, there has only been one human quite like that. True, some of the followers come closer than others, but by-and-large, our task is a simple one in this respect. Those recovering alcoholics keep trying to turn their lives and will over to the Enemy's care, but then they keep taking it back. You do not even have to do that much in the way of encouragement, which makes your whining letter to me all the more despicable.

If your client seems to be making progress on this new resolve of his, though I doubt he will, your task is still relatively simple. Let him have some successes. Let him come to feel that things are going well. Let him even congratulate himself on not drinking and going to meetings. At some point, plant the idea in his head that he is not doing so badly after all. Perhaps he was never really as bad as he thought. Those sorts of things. As Simon starts to feel better and gain more confidence, lead him to think that since he is on the right track again, he's not going to mess up—if only he watches himself carefully. In fact, get him to think carefully about his future life: plan for it, envision it; craft the illusions of how it will be for him. Then, when he has his images all in place—more in the future than in the present—you will have primed him for his downfall. Once again, he will think that his life is his business, instead of realizing that he is only the administrator, not the master. The human who has really surrendered to the Enemy can truly say "my life is not my business, but Yours." You will meet very few who can say this.

As Simon develops a new confidence, helped along by you, slowly implant the idea that it really would be all right to have an occasional drink again, just a beer or two or a glass of wine. He will be on guard against any temptation toward a major binge. If you have done your job right, he will have confidence in himself that he has now learned "how to handle it." Do not rush this too fast; you want to seduce him away from Him and into himself. He does not yet entirely understand the nature of his disease and doesn't really want to understand it. Blind Simon to any real insights in this respect. Pick a moment carefully and encourage him to have just one drink, and then encourage him to stop; give him great resolve to stop. You may be inclined, wrongly of course, to argue with me here. You probably think with Simon that you should encourage him to rush right back into heavy drinking. No. Instead, play him slowly, a few drinks over many days, but not enough to arouse his defenses. Let him think that, in fact, he does have it under control, never realizing that it is your effort that is giving him the most help. Within a few weeks, I believe that you will have him thoroughly hooked and then his defenses against heavy drinking will have been carefully weakened. Slow seductions are always more to my taste. I think that you will find his subsequent misery, once he realizes that he is drinking more than he did before he quit, quite to your liking.

One more thing. Give up on the idea of always having a mortal's will in our grave. It is not necessary to do that to break a being, and it is a waste of your time to spend too much energy on just one person. Simon will undoubtedly be trying to improve his conscious contact with God. If you can cleverly lead him back to the bottle he will probably convince himself, with your nasty assistance, that God has let him down. How many times have we seen a person with an alcohol problem say a token prayer—or even a heartfelt one—to the Enemy, asking His assistance in stopping drinking. Then, five minutes later, they are pouring themselves a drink! It is as if they expect the Creator to reach down and take the bottle out of their hand! If I had not seen this same scene replayed millions of times, I would not believe it myself. He will do for them what they cannot do for themselves, as those infernal AA maggots believe, but He won't do for them what they can do for themselves. Fortunately, most humans never learn this, so our task is easier.

I think that you can count on Simon to blame the Enemy for his own decision to start drinking again. Blind him, as best you can, to the truth of this; encourage him to resent God for making him the way he is. The Enemy will continue to love him nonetheless, but in his state he won't know it.

Sincerely,
Screwtape

Letter 16

Dear Rotbranch,

Through no fault of my own you were not given adequate preparation in the bedevilment of families of alcoholics. This failure lies directly with your instructors, and it is they who shall be punished. This omission in your training would not have been so important years ago when families of alcoholics were expected to be long-suffering and little else. However, now that more and more people are catching on to the chaos we help to create in such families, we must examine our strategies.

I will review the older approach because there are still many, many families for whom this is more than sufficient for our purposes. Most families develop patterns in how people interact with each other, and each member will have a special place. Families with alcoholics are no different in this respect. Someone will probably be bossy, someone will be more of the counselor type, someone will be the achiever, or whiner, and so forth. In short, each person will, in order to find a place, carve out a niche in which to specialize. Rarely will they realize this, of course.

In situations where the father has the alcoholism disease, we have helped to craft the place which each person fills. Wives can be counted on most of the time to become the "enablers," in their parlance. They will make the excuses, do all the necessary covering-up to keep the family secret, protect the husbands from the consequences of their drinking. In short, the enabling wife will assume responsibility for his life and carry that particular burden. Most, acting out of loving kindness (sometimes, embarrassment or fear), do not realize the great harm they are doing by assuming that kind of responsibility. They make it easier for the husbands to continue their behavior and avoid responsibility for themselves. There is an added benefit to us which is equally valuable. Since very few wives are true saints, you can nurture their resentment, self-pity and pain almost endlessly.

Children, too, can be easily moved into a warped place. Some child will get to be the hero of the family through their special achievements; it might be in school or sports or music—it really does not matter. The hero child will have the place of bringing a sense of value to the family, someone the family can be proud of. However, the hero child also tries, harder and ever harder, to compensate for the pains of the family. Such a child will, of course, always fail; you can work on the sense of failure to bring much misery. One of the children is likely to become a "lost" child, seeming to have no special place but, in fact, having the place of fading into the background. This child will be no trouble to the family, will indeed almost slip out of mind. I am sure you can see the opportunities here to corrode relationships. The lost child will find safety in being a "nobody," and getting close to no one. Since this pattern is so antithetical to their normal human needs, such children can be manipulated into great unhappiness, particularly later in life. Self-esteem can only grow in relationship with others; deprive a child of such healthy relationships and we can use the torment for years.

Perhaps my personal favorite is the black sheep or family scapegoat; I feel a special affinity with this one. A child in this place is really a distraction for the family. If the parent's alcoholism is a family secret, then the role of the scapegoat is to be the apparent problem for the family, the trouble-maker or malcontent. Such a child might be a trouble-maker at school, or get into trouble with the law, or be a source of trouble at home. Whatever it is does not really matter that much. What matters is that the family perceives this child as "the" problem, thereby distracting themselves from the pressing problem of alcoholism.

I remind you that all families will develop problems which help shape the place into which each member will fit. In some ways, alcoholic families are more fortunate since theirs is a relatively more visible disease. Others, and I say this with no small amount of amusement, are less conspicuous and therefore even less prone to get help for the problems. Families with chronic depressives, or rage-aholics or religious fanatics are just a few which come to mind; there are so many, many more for our table.

Some of these humans have contrived the concept of dysfunctional family, another label which will pass out of fad status sooner rather than later. To them, any dysfunctional family is one which has serious problems so that healthy development is stunted. As if it has ever been another way! These creatures have such a glamorized view of families in the past that they feel further deprived by the current state of things. Fools! There is, however, an outside chance that much will come of the current trend to recognize and do something about serious family problems, so we must be particularly offensive.

As you know, we are not privileged to see the future as is He; not even Our Father Below has that capacity. The recent tide of treating whole families when one has alcoholism was not anticipated by our forecasters. We had so long counted on the human tendency to label and judge just one person as the problem in the family that our forecasters became careless. (Needless to say, they no longer are.) It is to our great disadvantage when whole families cooperate in the recovery process of the alcoholic. Much is undone. Not only does the one with the disease have a better chance of recovery, but we then have to combat the healing of the other family members as well. God has blind-sided us with this development, but do not become discouraged. So few families ever rally round like this that we do not lose all that much.

As usual, there is always opportunity for you to spread destruction and decay if you are cunning. Your first strategy is always to block any efforts at individual recovery; barring that you should abort any inclination of the family to join in the recovery efforts. Lead them to think that it is only the problem of the alcoholic member. Nurture their judgmentalism and feed their personal fears of change. It is a great loss to us when He, using the disease of a single member, is able to bring about healing of several people all at once.

For those people who have come to understand the concept of being in a dysfunctional family, your best avenue is to keep them trapped within themselves. Lead them into a mental quicksand of trying to relate everything in their lives to their family's dysfunction. Encourage them to overanalyze, overscrutinize, overexamine and understand everything from that one vantage point. Ignorance may not have been bliss for many of them, but knowledge will be no better if it can be distorted for our purposes. As long as you can keep them mired in their own thinking about why they are the way they are, you can quite effectively abort real change. If nothing else, lead them to feel resentful that *they* have been in a less than healthy family.

Humans love to have something on which to blame their lives; they then have lifetime excuses for not being responsible for their own choices. Use this tendency for Our Father Below.

Yours sincerely,
Screwtape

Letter 17

Dear Rotbranch,

Past and present evil are never enough; you must always be on the lookout for more opportunities to bring the agony of souls to our banquet. We do not have the same power as the Enemy and have to work incessantly for our sustenance. Do not rest, ever.

I have noticed, from information reaching me from a variety of sources (did you think I know your work only from you?), that you have been staggeringly idle in using alcohol to provoke violent outbursts in the souls assigned to you. What possible excuse could you have for ignoring this arena of destruction? You know damn well that alcohol usage produces chemical changes in human brains, and that many humans with a proclivity for control or anger are especially susceptible to alcoholic rages. Have you totally forgotten this aspect of your training?

Certainly you can induce some of your clients to have violent outbursts. In some human societies, mortals are so ready to strike out at those they love when their wishes or control needs are being threatened that you don't even have to do very much. Alcoholic humans in these same societies are even more susceptible and should be child's play in your hands. Many humans believe it is morally wrong to hit a wife or child or anyone else;

many others have no such belief or, if they do, it is easily overcome by their angry impulses or diverted by us. While He gave
them the gift of anger for good reasons, most of them can be led
to misuse it for their own selfish purposes, if we do our work
right. Even His Son was angry at times, although always, of
course, in service of the Enemy. Curse Him forever.

One of the primary attractions of alcohol use to many humans is that it lowers their inhibitions, allows them to be more
free than they feel. They want to be someone other than who
they are. Shy people can temporarily overcome shyness, fearful
people temporarily overcome their fears. Angry people can become more mellow—up to a point. You should have ample opportunity with those who have strong control needs or angry impulses to drink beyond their safe point; those with the disease
should be easily manipulated to violence. Let them beat their
wives, their girlfriends, their children—whoever they proclaim to
love. However, help them to avoid getting into physical confron-
tations, when they are under the influence of alcohol, with
friends or strangers. They are less likely to get away with it and
might actually learn something.

Most human relationships, particularly intimate ones, will
carry an accumulation of irritations, aggravations and sometimes outright hostilities if you do your work well. When drinking, these mortals will not have as much control over their impulses, angry or otherwise. There is nothing, save for the
Enemy, to prevent you from leading at least some of them to
lash out violently. Then, hours or days later, let them be apologetic, full of apparent sorrow for what they have done, making a
thousand hollow promises that it will never happen again. Lead
them to *blame the alcohol*, proclaiming with the deepest of sin-
cerity that it would not have happened if they had not been
drinking. With some devilish preparation, you can even blind
some of them to the truth so they actually believe what they are
saying! They have thus deceived themselves (always to our advantage) by blaming something external for what is an inner
defect; men are particularly good at this.

The tastiness of the strategy is that, again with careful preparation, you can get wives to believe the lie as well. Many men don't entirely know that they are lying because it is too much trouble for them to look beyond the surface of their souls to see the truth. But many do know the lie. No matter. Women have been well trained to deny the truth, and want to believe that this person who has beaten her really would not have done it if he had not been drinking. The fact that such abuse occurs very often when he is not drinking does not seem to enter their logic, so determined are they to believe that their loved one couldn't really want to hurt them. A lovely meal, is it not? Help them to justify the violence with alcohol and let it become an excuse for behavior that would not be tolerated outside family relationships.

You need not limit yourself to violent physical outbursts; some humans will be resistant to your temptations in this area, and you would waste your time. Instead, you can often accomplish even more destruction with verbal and psychological violence. Many humans can go along for years without quite realizing—if you keep them blind—that what they are really feeling is a crumbling of their spirits, the effects of a barrage of abuse. I am particularly fond of this approach because healing is ever so much slower than it is for a broken nose or arm! Since they can see neither the damage nor the scars, they can ignore the consequences for years while you spread the decay.

Since He also gave them the gift of speech, let us warp this to our own ends and cause Him anguish. Lead them to use speech as a weapon, hurling words against another which slam and pummel and flatten the spirit. Hateful, demeaning words. Destructive and vicious words. Words which eat and wither their spirits. Words which kill and enshroud their self-esteem. You can do it!

There is ample opportunity to do this with both men and women. Since the latter tend toward greater subtlety, you can amuse yourself by toying with just the right combination of minimum viciousness to produce the most damage. Both husbands and children will be quite susceptible. An added garnish to this dish is that few men will admit to having their feelings hurt, much less badly wounded; they will either cover the hurt with anger or carry it around for years. Either can be quite satisfactory in rotting the relationships. Use the same strategy with verbal violence as I instructed with physical assaults. Lead them to be apologetic for what they have said, contrite that they could have been so mean. Let them blame it all on the alcohol, believing that that is the cause.

I do hope that you are catching onto this strategy, for it is one of our best for self-deception and the prolonged deterioration of mortal relationships. Humans would far rather have an excuse for what they do and say than ever admit to themselves— let alone another—that there is any hatefulness in their hearts. All action is preceded by thought (why don't they realize this?). If they carry around aggrieved, angry or resentful thoughts long enough, they are likely to explode. See to it that their explosions are directed toward those they love.

Even when you cannot lead them to a destructive explosion, it is sometimes just as well. Grievances held in their hearts long enough will wreak havoc on their spirits as well as their bodies. The human machine cannot physically withstand years of inner pain without breaking down in some way. Obviously, it is always more to our advantage to let the spirit suffocate than the body suffer; they pay more attention to the latter.

Sincerely,
Screwtape

Letter 18

Dear Rotbranch,

You have promoted fruitful afflictions in many of your clients, but I believe that you could be doing much better with the men assigned to your perdition. It is my distinct impression that some of them are getting dangerously close to forming wholesome relationships with other men in their recovery programs. You must be vigilant in undermining any efforts men make to do this. We must abort decent human relationships, using any avenue at our disposal.

Thanks to some of your predecessors, we have been quite successful in this century in distorting men's relationships with other men. There is great advantage to us in this. As long as men really cannot relate very well to other men, it leads them to look to women to solve their problems, comfort them incessantly, stroke their egos, make them feel good about themselves. In short, their perceived inaccessibility of other men leads them to use women for their own selfish purposes. The fact that women seldom get back what they put into a friendship with a man also contributes to our cause; while we get men to act on their selfish side, we get to kindle progressive disappointments and resentments in women. A pleasant spread, would you not agree?

There is always the opportunity, with a little help from our side, that what could be a solid friendship will become sexualized, and hence the friendship with a woman is changed forever. It does not take much encouragement, as you well know, to lead a man to start having sexual thoughts about someone who, up to that point, had been a good friend to him. If men learned to take such thoughts in stride, or even to laugh at them instead of acting on them, we would have far fewer opportunities. Humans often feel a special attraction when there is a shared spiritual bond between them, a fact which still mystifies many of them. When will they ever learn (never, if we work hard) that both sexuality and spirituality, when healthy, share the common thread of oneness, and that they are innately drawn to oneness? Oneness is where they originated. Thanks to our cunning, we can often deform this for our purposes and pervert the original intention.

I see that I have digressed; let me return to my original point. There are other advantages in warping men's relationships with other men. As long as we help perpetuate this, we effectively cut men off from half of the human race. I have known many great successes in my day, but this one is among the most heinous; basically unable to relate to other men in a healthy way and predisposed to relating to women in self-centered ways, men often have almost no one with whom they have easy friendships. That cursed human, C. S. Lewis, considered friendships to be the most angelic of the four loves, and he was right—when they are healthy. If we continue to do our work carefully, most men will never achieve good friendships with other men. Undoubtedly you see the other main advantage to us here. As long as we can lead men to have great difficulty in developing good relationships with other men, there is less chance that they will develop a healthy masculinity. As it is now the concept is so misshapen that even men who are trying hard to do this have a confusing time. Continue to build on the work of your predecessors and we shall have ample feasts for the future.

One of the many hazards of recovery programs is that men will finally begin to share their inner selves with other men, guardedly at first and then, with increasing confidence, at ever deeper levels. I need not remind you that this is exceedingly dangerous for our designs and you must circumvent this wherever possible. We do not want men to discover that other men have the same fears, anxieties and apprehensions that they do. We do not want them to realize that their innermost struggles are shared by others. If they must talk together, try to keep the talk confined to how awful they were when they were drinking. It is entertaining to lead them to regale each other with their drunken exploits, not realizing that they are playing the typical male game of competing with each other. Deep down, where you can see but many of them will not look, men often have about the same problems with self-esteem which women do. We have been infinitely more successful with men in getting them to cover this up with false confidence, phony self-assurance and a defensive assertiveness. While they think that they are acting like "real men" are expected to act, they may sense, deep down that something is quite amiss; they will feel a hollowness where they expect to find strength. We have well crafted their inclination to look to women to fill this hollow, which women, of course cannot do.

As usual, our cursed Enemy stands ready to help them in any of their needs, eager and excited like some damnable parent watching a child take the first steps. Happily for us, it does not occur to men very often to ask the Creator for help in their male relationships. Oh, they'll plead about jobs, and drinking, and girlfriends and all sorts of other things which involve fears and worries. It simply seems not to occur to them that He who created all might be interested in helping them in this area. Try to keep it that way. The same man who, as a boy would defiantly proclaim "ha, ha, it doesn't hurt," will be highly resistant to admitting to any man, ever, "I hurt."

Persuade them to be apprehensive and fearful about disclosing to other men any of their fears and insecurities which might embody their sense of masculinity. If they have a thought about disclosing something painful in a meeting, remind them how weak it will make them look to other men. If they are inclined to call a male friend to talk, lead them to think that they should be able to handle it, they should be able to handle anything. Lead them to think that if they were only stronger as a man, they wouldn't need to reach out for help.

I believe that if you pursue these strategies you can successfully retard men's recovery, lead them to misuse women, and deprive the Enemy of one way they might turn their lives over to Him. If you take the offensive, it will not occur to men that their thinking and feelings about male friendships, distorted by the effects of the disease and a sick society, might be in need of healing. Nonalcoholics are not much better, of course, but that is not your assignment. If we can prevent men from loving other men in any healthy spiritual way, we will have accomplished a great deal in limiting how well they can love themselves. They might wholeheartedly practice the Enemy's injunction to "love your neighbor"; lead them to forget the other half, "as yourself."

Sincerely,
Screwtape

Letter 19

Dear Rotbranch,

You fool! Ruth is onto you. Why did you not see that? Your last letter to me was filled with loathsome whining. You say you try to get her to not pray, and she prays all the more. You try to get her to skip going to recovery meetings with a variety of rationalizations, and she goes to even more meetings. You try to get her to isolate herself, and she makes even more phone calls than she had been doing before you initiated these efforts. How could you be so blind as to miss this? She knows what you are up to! I don't have enough information to know if this is an unusually perceptive and spiritually-attuned woman, or if you have just been unusually careless in your management of this client. You had best hope that I never find out it has been the latter.

I am quite confident that your teachers more than adequately discussed the variation in humans and the need to tempt according to their personalities and where they are on their spiritual path. With some you can be blatantly present in their thoughts and they will never suspect a thing. With others you cannot go blundering into their thoughts as if they were spiritual fools; do this and you instantly drive them closer to the God we loathe. Frankly, I suspect that you have made a great error with Ruth and it will take some time to correct.

You are never helpless. You need to modify strategies according to her apparent disposition. From what you have told me earlier about Ruth, it appears that she has sincerely embraced the recovery effort and is unlikely to be easily tempted back to the bottle. She sees what pain she has brought into her own life, her husband's and her children's. She has made promises, heartfelt, I am sorry to see, that she is really trying to get well. It is to my everlasting regret that she now sees herself as a sick person trying to get well instead of a bad person trying to get good. The latter suits our purposes much better, as it does for all mortals with alcohol problems. As long as we can maintain their beliefs in themselves as fundamentally bad, we can keep them distant from the Enemy and from genuine sharing of themselves in human relationships.

I believe, and certainly I am right in this, that you need to nurture her involvement with the program of recovery, but lead her to overdo everything. These people are fond of saying that their sobriety comes first, and will let nothing stand in their way. Fine. See that nothing stands in Ruth's way of going to meetings, making new friends, spending more and more time with people outside of her family. Let her believe that she is doing well by her devotion to her program, and blind her to her compulsion to "do it perfectly." She so wants to get well that she only pays lip service to the AA motto of seeking progress rather than perfection. In her heart of hearts she wants to make amazing progress, to prove to herself, to her family, to her friends, to the world that she really is a completely new person. Never mind that she will always have some defects; she wants to believe that if only she works the program just right, she will never have any future temptation to drink. We know better.

After awhile her family will start to protest that they never see her anymore, that she spends time with her new friends but not with them, that they had such high hopes as a new family—but it just doesn't feel right to them now. Ruth will probably suspect that they are right but, fearful of letting up in her recovery efforts (if you have done your job right), she will stifle their protests and defend what she is doing. If she starts to have any persistent thought that they are right, remind her of how much happier and freer she has become since beginning recovery. Remind her that they just don't understand. Remind her that only her new friends really know what she is going through. In short, lead her into an all-or-none frame of mind.

Humans often confuse the means with the end, and Ruth is no exception. Let her think of the program as an end in itself instead of just a tool for her to use in her recovery efforts. Let her think that someday she will be able to spend a normal amount of time with her family, but not until everything is under control. Let her become as obsessed with meetings and her new friends as she once was obsessed with alcohol. The Creator takes away the alcohol obsession and even the desire from so many of the humans that they often cannot remember what it was like when their days revolved around when they would have their first drink. Ruth remembers this in her head, but since she no longer feels the compulsion, she is open to new compulsions. I am quite optimistic that this strategy will work with her. Her family relationships will not be as bad as they had been, but you can keep them quite disrupted nonetheless. Since her husband and children had such high hopes of what their family life would be like after she began recovery, they will soon become disheartened. Anytime you can *dis*hearten an entire family, you receive great credit from Our Father Below.

The family will be afraid, for quite awhile, to press their complaints very hard, lest they upset her recovery. This is an opportune time to create fresh resentments and no small amount of guilt. Her family will want to be totally supportive and simply not know what to do; try to keep them in this state of confusion as long as possible. The dashing of human hopes is quite delicious; I am sure you will enjoy it.

> Sincerely,
> Screwtape

Letter 20

Dear Rotbranch,

I appreciate your raising the issue of lust in your last letter, and you are quite correct in your view that this game has changed considerably during this century.

Certainly you will recall from your introductory classes that the Creator provided humans with a sexual instinct, although why He should bestow such a powerfully wonderful gift upon these miserable creatures is beyond me. I have always considered the past human explanation about such instinct being solely for reproduction to be far too pat an answer, and rather myopic at that. It is almost as if His infinite Goodness *wants* these beings to have moments of great intimacy and pleasure. Since none of ours can possibly understand the concept of wanting good for the human beasts, there will always be a mystery.

Some mortals believe that all sexual appetite is wrong. That is fine for our purposes since it is such a decisive rejection of one of the Creator's gifts. Anytime we can lead them to reject one of His gifts we have gained a victory. With this particular group we have little to worry about in the sexual regard.

Some of your predecessors have achieved spectacular and atrocious success in creating a hedonistic milieu in many cultures of the 20th century. Many humans have become wonderfully confused about sexual matters and have opted for the easy way out. Their motto is, "if it feels good, do it!" Another of our successes. The mortal propensity for excess has worked greatly to our advantage as we have twisted His basic gift into a kind of sexual entitlement. Responsibility, commitment, true intimacy and meaning are easily set aside for the sake of simple carnal satisfactions. Were Midas still alive, he would be envious that he had not thought of hoarding sexual excess.

Humans with alcoholism are no different in their sexual instincts from others. Rather, those with the disease—men more so than women—can be led to cultivate a good many habits of sexual selfishness as a specific form of self-seeking. Alcoholics always want to feel differently than they do. If they feel bad, they want to feel good. If they feel good, they want to feel better. If they feel better, they want to hoard the feeling so they always have a source. It is scarcely different than their vigilance in as-suring that they are never without a supply of alcohol. Recall your instruction that alcoholism is a disease of thinking and feel-ing as much, perhaps more, as a disease of alcohol dependence.

Your role is to nurture their dissatisfaction: how they feel, think, and think about how they feel. A tasty torment, is it not? Lead them into the temptation of self-preoccupation where their feelings and thinking become hopelessly entangled; and then, implant the idea of how they can feel better. With active alcohol-ics you will have to do nothing to encourage drinking, even bet-ter if it is getting loaded with someone of the opposite sex. Twist their temptations together and you will accomplish much more. With those in recovery programs, it is quite acceptable with some to ignore the drinking path.

Either group can be turned to their lustful sides. Men in particular are prone to sexual excess in their thinking, even when it is not acted out. If you let their sexual appetites stay at a slow simmer, you can bring much disruption to their serenity. Lead them to the pleasure of sexual fantasies, to be constantly filled with appetite for that which is bad for them, careless and meaningless liaisons, for example. One of the surest ways to lead a man back to the bottle is to engage his sexual energies in pursuit of dishonesty. Lead him to think that he is genuinely interested in a particular woman and, armed with this rationalization, ignore the fact that virtually any woman would do. Let him think that he is harming no one when he enters into a brief liaison. Since he will not want to face the truth that all action has consequences, it will be relatively easy for you to lead him to dupe himself. Let him always be on the alert for new objects for his sexual fantasy projections.

The achievement of these objectives will keep men in a state of agitation, which makes both serenity and prayer more difficult. They will resist turning over their lust to the Enemy, fearing that if they do so they will somehow be weakened and emasculated—as if He is going to remove the basic instinct! They like the energy and, in fact, are often addicted to the adrenaline charge which accompanies the pursuit and conquest of a woman. (Often, the actual conquest is less of a stimulation to them than the hunt). This is excellent for our purposes because they can then convince themselves—with our help, of course—that there was some flaw in the woman and the next one, or the next, will be just right for them.

You can expect to encounter a more difficult challenge in warping women's sexual instincts. Where most societies give men almost free sexual license, the same societies have developed far more restrictions for women. Although this is changing slowly in some cultures, women do not have as much permission to go on the hunt as do men. Your best avenue with women is to lead them to feel that they must be wanted, must be needed, must be held—all by a man, of course—in order to be happy. Lead women to believe and *feel* how much better their lives would be if only they had a man. Since few men are going to maintain a platonic relationship, it can easily be sexualized. He gets what he wants, with no commitment, and she settles for less than she wanted in order to get something, someone.

Some women, of course, will feel far less sexually restricted. Some will be "on the hunt" as much as any man. Your task with such a mortal is to assure that the men she attracts are invariably bad for her: demeaning, degrading and full of selfishness. With so many women hope, indeed, does spring eternal. Toy with her unhealthy affections, prolong her illusions despite all evidence to the contrary, and then enjoy the feast when you smash all hope for a wholesome and enduring relationship. Both her ego and spirit will then be so wounded that you can work all manner of evil with shame and guilt.

I remind you again that alcoholics have the same instincts as do all humans, there is nothing you can do about that. Your task is to distort the gift for our purposes, confuse their thinking, impair their judgment and blind their wisdom. With careful and sustained bedevilment you can entrap many men and women into quite sick relationships and keep them there for years. Bon appétit.

Sincerely,
Screwtape

Letter 21

Dear Rotbranch,

Brilliant! Cunning! Diabolically brilliant! Your occasional flair for evil genius reminds me of myself.

You won the holiday through cleverness, cunning and control. Oh, how I wish I had been there! You knew that Susanna would be having many thoughts about drinking during the holiday, especially around that family of hers. You were correct and ever so cunning to leave unchallenged her resolve not to drink. A lesser devil might have tried to do battle with her obvious determination, only to lose everything. But you, my foul Rotbranch, were wise enough to let her have her way with not drinking. I have to give you extra credit for making sure everyone around her was having such a good time, an unusually festive time at that. Then! Then, to plant that tiny little seed for her to feel sorry for herself, to resent deep down that everyone else could drink and she could not! Genius! I can tell that your very long training period is reaping fine rewards for us.

What twists these humans can do within themselves. Susanna could have spent the day, as we might have feared, in gratitude to our Enemy that she was given the strength to defeat her active drinking. Or, perish the saving thought, she could have seen the grace of her resolve early in the day and recognized the damnable blessings being poured into her life. All this makes your victory much the more satisfying. You enabled her to spend the day in self-pity, cut off not only from her recognition of blessings and grace, but secretly harboring anger and resentment that everyone else was having such a good time when she was not.

Recovery is a harder road for her to travel right now since so many of her immediate family are active drinkers, but none have the disease of alcoholism. It is very difficult for her to understand why she alone is not free to drink like the others. She desperately wants to understand—which, to her, means that it makes sense to her. Since it will never be given to her to know the why of her difference, you may be able to keep her entrapped in resentment, not only for the disease but also for understanding eluding her. She will then, quite naturally, feel cheated on both accounts. If you do your work right, she will never become grateful for the disease, will never be able to laugh at it or herself. On the one hand, she wants to be like everyone else, but on the other hand she wants to be special—but special in the ways of her choosing, not the Creator's.

I think that you have done a laudable job in making her family less than understanding. They no longer nag her to join them in their drinks, but they often look at her as if to say "just one won't hurt!" Susanna now knows better, knows that the first drink she takes will set her on the path to a drunk, knows that she can never drink again. And yet, if you persist in your affliction, she will hold onto that dangerous hope that so many with the disease embrace: one day she will be able to drink normally. When her family looks at her, it is as if to say "you *can* control your drinking with will power," and the look always makes her heart ache because she knows better. One day her family might truly understand that she is different, that she has a disease which they do not have, and become more empathetic. Try to delay that day for as long as possible.

I do not want to overload you with praise at this success for I would not want you to get sloppy in your work. It is never-ending work, and the minute you become less persistent, the Enemy has even greater leverage and control. You must never, ever forget that His guidance is something that these recovering alcoholics say they want. True, it is easy enough to turn them away from their puny resolves by giving them an especially bad day or an especially good one, but the line of attack is not always best pursued along their drinking addictions.

As you have learned with this victory over Susanna, the human capacity for self-congratulation is equaled only by their reservoir of self-pity if even little things do not go their way. It is, I suppose, fortunate for us because it provides so many avenues of destruction. The Enemy, damn Him forever, is immensely forgiving, even when they offer and take back their will like some spiritual yo-yo. Her lukewarm holiday, wrapped within an honest anger and an unfelt appreciation, is sure to weigh heavily on her mind. Encourage her to remember the many holidays when she was drinking, but enable her to suppress the painful parts so that she glamorizes the past. She will then have a totally unreal comparison: her fantasied holidays of the past with the tepid holidays that she now envisions stretching interminably into the future. Try to keep her locked into this comparison for as long as possible, for it will make her future (and therefore her spirit) bleak. Humans have precious little ability to live just in the present, and spend far more of their time thinking about what has already happened or what might happen in the future. Part of your job is to nurse this inclination for our benefit. Divert her attention if she starts to have any thoughts that, in time, she will have joyful and sober holidays. Instead, let her project all future holidays to be the same as this one, tepid and uncomfortable.

Perhaps with a bit of continued cunning you can help Susanna begin to think that she is really better off not being around her family at all. Isolate her successfully and she will be much more vulnerable to our temptations.

Sincerely yours,
Screwtape

(Note to courier: report back to me immediately after delivering this to Rotbranch. This woman should be child's play in his hands and he is barely winning the battle).

Letter 22

Dear Rotbranch,

This is the final time I shall review for you anything basic about human temperament and temptation! Your questions convince me that you have not learned the rudiments at all well and lead me to surmise that some of your classmates would be far more suited to the evil which you are allegedly doing. I guarantee you, this is the last time. Any further evidence of ignorance on your part will result in your end; as you know, there are no appeals.

For thousands of years we have helped to hone human temperament and tailored our temptations to fit. All humans have a basic predisposition, an Achilles heel of their wretched souls. Those with alcohol problems are no different. If you do not first attempt to corrupt their spirits through the particular human's weak point, you are wasting time. Since it is not given to us to know when the Kingdom will come, we can afford to waste no time. Any victory for us is a loss to the Enemy. You must master this material and direct it against the souls in your charge.

Some mortals are inclined to speak of these weak points as deadly sins; some of them refer to them as compulsions, others call them by different names. No matter. Humans have all of these characteristics to some degree, but each has a particular weak point. It is your job to quickly discern the weak point and there apply the pressure. For those with alcohol problems your task is simple: find their particular spiritual weak point (or sin, if you would rather call it that) and determine how to best use alcohol to exacerbate the weakness. Any fool knows that the best way to promote rot is to find the least healthy part of the creature and encourage corruption to spread. Never forget, however, that it is precisely at these weak spots that the Creator is most likely to be found trying to heal. He uses their weaknesses to bring them to Him.

For your review, the weak spots are anger, pride, vanity, envy, greed, fear, gluttony, lust, and sloth. While each human has all of these to some degree, one will predominate—as a sinister magnet in the core of their spirits. Your rapid perception of the Achilles heel in a particular human is essential so you do not waste time attacking that part of their soul which is essentially healthy and strong and thus less vulnerable to your corruptions.

Fortunately for us, most of them do not know their true weak spots and tend to confuse superficial personality problems with spiritual compulsions. In fact, most humans will spend their entire lives in avoidance of the truth about their core weakness. They will develop thinking and behavior patterns in reaction to these compulsions, but will never realize what they are doing. Your job is to keep it that way. As usual, blind them to the truth about themselves. Be particularly wary of the recent and rapid spread in interest in the enneagram; this development does not bode well for us. Some humans make the choice to pursue this approach to spiritual understanding, knowing that the process will strip away their false egos. I need not remind you of the danger to our designs when humans start looking at the core of their souls very closely.

Once you have located your client's compulsion, then utilize the alcohol dependency to feed the weakness. Encourage the person to imagine any recovery possibility through the view of their weak point; you thus greatly diminish the likelihood that recovery and real spiritual growth will take place. For instance, if a man you are working with has the compulsion of lust, let him imagine that recovery will mean an end to his exuberance for life, let him see the future without alcohol as one lacking in vitality, let him see the spiritual life as passionless. Do not make the mistake of thinking that those with this compulsion are particularly sexual; rather, their drive is the passion for excess, to feel everything strongly. If your client happens to be a woman with the compulsion of envy, let her see an alcohol-free life as one of ordinariness. Since she is inclined to want to see herself as special, she will resist any change which might deprive her of this quality. You may have a client whose weak spot is sloth; afflict them with inertia and you will keep them within your snare. Recovery from the alcohol addiction is simple, but it is not easy (thanks in part to us). Let the slothful client imagine how much trouble it will be to go to meetings, to change his ways and the way he interacts with others. In short, let him imagine recovery as more trouble than he is willing to bear and always, always, lead your client to forget that all he has to do is make the effort; the result is up to Him. You will have many clients who have the fear compulsion; in particular you will find them among the workaholics of the world. These people often cope with their fears (which they will not recognize if you do your work properly) by overwork, by constantly pursuing great successes, by being in control of everything that comes into their lives. Those who have this weak point can best be approached by feeding their fears: make them afraid to change their drinking, afraid to face themselves, afraid to admit to any weakness. Virtually all alcoholics have viewed the disease as weakness rather than disease, and it is to our advantage to maintain this perception, particularly among those with the fear compulsion.

I am guardedly confident that you can deduce the proper approach regardless of your client's particular temperament, and will shape the temptation to fit. It is imperative to remember that the God who made them has His own purposes which we must counter at every turn. He seems to use their weaknesses as an avenue to heal their souls and draw them closer. He does this by letting them see themselves as they really are; and then, enlightened by His grace, they finally learn to love themselves just as they are. I cringe when I think of the multitude of times we have thought to have a mortal well in our grasp and He, using the very weakness we have nurtured, gives them the grace of insight. Their weakness provides the impetus for recovery and return to Him.

Most humans will quite naturally wish to avoid peering very deeply into their souls; strive to encourage their apprehensions about this, for insight always brings the risk of revelation. The more we can encourage them in self-deception, the better. Humans are, by nature, basically spiritually lazy and wish to do no more than is necessary in order to "get into heaven." Deep in their souls they know that God wants them to be wholehearted within themselves and in pursuit of Him. Our task is to keep them halfhearted, ignorant and disinclined to face themselves exactly as they are. Should they have the stirrings of such self-examination, do your best to divert these with their weak points. Humans often think worse of themselves than they really are, and fear ever really seeing their exposed souls; feed these fears.

It is greatly to our advantage that they do not know the rejoicing that their simple acts of kindness and humility bring to the Creator. Deprived of divine realization that there is much good about them as seen through His eyes, they are often inclined to see themselves as we would have them be: full of soulrot. Encourage this.

Sincerely,
Screwtape

Letter 23

Dear Rotbranch,

It was good to receive your last letter and to learn of your successes with Daniel and Judith. It is wonderful to have the opportunity to bedevil a married couple with the same temptations; the satisfaction and amusement are unparalleled. I particularly relished your description of their struggles to maintain a loving relationship in the face of their adversities, and imagine that your appetite has stayed well stimulated.

Permit me—I'm sure you will not object—to offer some advice which may assist your efforts in increasing their anguish. From everything you have told me about them, I deduce that their joint efforts at recovery from their addictions have gotten off to a shaky start. Each seems to be looking to the other for support and encouragement to handle their loss of alcohol on top of their other losses. I know that you did not have anything to do with her father's death, nor with Daniel losing his job. Nonetheless, you can use these developments to push them where we want them.

At this point I probably would not even bother with many temptations to drink, although if you think otherwise, you are free to pursue this course. Rather, I think that there is more to be gained by contorting their sorrows into self-pity. They will then be overly focused on and within themselves, a perfect spot for our afflictions.

Humans have the sentiment of sorrow, which we can neither know nor experience. It seems to be an aching feeling that grows in their hearts when they are facing the loss of something of value that they are attached to; the attachment might be a person, an opportunity, a vision, or something else. The sentiment appears to be much the same, regardless of what it is they cherished. Sorrow itself is a healthy emotion and therefore not much use to us. Only He knows why they have it; perhaps it is to act as a balance to the joy which He wants them to have in abundance. As near as we can deduce, the Enemy wants these creatures to live and love in freedom, but not to forget where their Home really will be found. Sorrow seems to play a role in the Creator's damnable plan to let them choose Him.

You always, always have the opportunity with humans to convert their sorrow into self-pity. If sorrow serves His purpose, then self-pity serves ours. Alcoholics in particular are very vulnerable to our temptations in this area. Since they have spent years relying on a drug to make them feel good, you can depend on them not having accepted the necessity of sorrow in their lives. Sorrow interferes with their goal of feeling good.

Try to discourage the sorrowful state, if for no other reason than the Creator often seems to be closest to them when they are so vulnerable. Instead, lead them away from their sorrowful thoughts and feelings and into themselves. When they are sorrowful, they are really focused outside themselves—on the lost person or vision or whatever. This is too beneficial for our purposes. If you are shrewd, you can twist their sorrow into self-pity. Self-pity traps them within themselves; it thus diminishes their relationships with other humans and with the Creator. It prevents any genuine gratitude (which we always must battle) because they will obsess about what they have lost or don't have, rather than think about all the gifts they've been given.

Self-pity has the added advantage, if you can maintain it long enough, of feeding upon itself. What might have started as a wholesome sorrow will, with your help, become a destructive self-pity about the present state of their lives. Bloat their self-pity by leading them to recall earlier disappointments and losses. Desiring to feel good, active alcoholics will rely ever more on the bottle; recovering alcoholics can much more easily be led back to drink and to our downward, hellish spiral.

Few humans have truly learned—thanks to monumental efforts on our part—that transformation is seldom possible without some sort of death: death of a dream, an image of self, a person. In their heads they understand the connection between death and resurrection, but in their hearts and guts are rarely able to apply this to their day-to-day lives. They think of transformation only as something which might happen at the conclusion of their lives on earth. Obviously, we want them to stay ignorant in this respect.

Continue to blind them to the necessity for little deaths along the way of their spiritual growth; let them treat these as cosmic cruelties and lead them into the feeling that life is, indeed, unfair. Abort any thoughts they might have to pray at the hours of these deaths. Let them pity themselves. Any day that their hearts do not praise Him is a victory for us.

With this couple your best strategy is to promote their self-pity. Let each of them feel, without disclosing to the other or to anyone who might name the temptation, that their own life is unduly harsh. Work on their human tendencies to want much more than they have. Bring into their memories the pain and adversities they have had to handle over the years of their marriage. If you want some real pleasure, lead each of them to think, in the privacy of their own thoughts, that they have had it much worse off than has their mate. Even though misery loves company, most humans like to think that their own agonies are somehow unique. You can feed this thought and, for many mortals, turn it into a bizarre source of pride. They will not be aware of this, of course. While you cannot let up with Judith and Daniel I believe that this course of action will certainly lead one or both of them back to drink. There is no rush on this; we can gain just as much by entrapping them in cycles of self-pity as we can by their return to active drinking.

At the same time, you must not let down your guard against the Enemy. You must blind them to the fact that what they are really feeling is self-pity rather than sorrow. Genuine sorrow can be redeeming; the self-pity that we want is enslaving. Enjoy this feast.

Sincerely,
Screwtape

Letter 24

Dear Rotbranch,

Your work with Martha is proceeding nicely, and I see by what you have written, and other reports coming to me, that you have managed to keep her restless and discontent. You have learned your lessons well.

Mortals can scarcely understand that another human may simply not have—and therefore cannot give—what it is they need or want that person to provide. They will end up feeling that the other is simply withholding from them, and take it entirely personally. If ever they could step outside of themselves long enough to realize how ludicrous is this expectation, perhaps they would make more rapid spiritual progress toward acceptance of others as they are.

Fortunately, we do not have to worry about this because they are seldom able to do it. Your work with Martha is a good case in point, and perhaps I shall use this in my next instruction with the devils in training. You were quite correct to let her feel better and better about herself for quitting drinking, quite right to not challenge her commitment to this at the present time. Perhaps you could have won that battle, but no matter. As we both know, there are bigger battles for her soul which must occupy our attention. Instead, what you have correctly done is to lead her to expect others around her to make changes because she herself is doing so. You insidiously stirred her inner tendencies to feel entitled to expect such changes: that her husband would finally be able to see her for the wonderful person that she feels herself to be, and freely give the understanding which she so desperately wants (and, I might add, deserves). You and I both know that her husband does not have this quality within himself, at least not to any degree that will register with her. He simply does not have real empathy as one of the gifts from our Enemy. Nonetheless, Martha keeps waiting for it, expecting it, feeling entitled to it. As she tries hard to be an understanding person, she feels that she should get what she gives, not really realizing that her gifts may not have been given to those closest to her.

I know that it did not take all that much effort for you to plant the seeds of discontent within her as she sees that empathy is not forthcoming. You have wisely blinded her to the possibility that she might use this opportunity for accepting her husband just as he is, a spiritual step forward which we must constantly guard against. It is best to not stir the resentment to the point of bitterness. In her case, you do not want her to be so filled with ill will that she realizes what is going on and turns to the Enemy for help. No; let her proceed as she is right now for awhile, vaguely disappointed, irritable and discontent. This will certainly block her relationship with her husband and with He whom we hate.

Perhaps it would be wise if you could introduce someone into her life that has exactly the qualities which she wants, a fellow church member or neighbor—the choice is up to you. Then, over the coming months she cannot help but make comparisons between this newfound friend and her husband who, while not a bad sort, simply cannot have all the qualities which she wants. Martha will be increasingly blind, if you work carefully, to the qualities which her husband does have which the new friend does not, and then feel that she has been cheated. Again, I urge you caution in her case because we do not want the attraction of friendship to become a romantic one. That development runs the risk of alerting her that you are at work in her life, and the less she suspects of your presence the better. Instead, let it remain a simple friendship, neither overly close nor distant. That way, Martha will constantly have the reminder of what her husband is not, and fail to appreciate him for what he is.

Acceptance, genuine acceptance, is very hard for humans; regardless of what they have, they almost always want more. When these wants are properly caressed by one of ours, then it is far easier to keep them in our grip. While you are afflicting her, remember to let her judge herself harshly for qualities she does not have, but wants. Goad her to use the same moldering lack of acceptance of herself as she has for her husband. Lead her to minimize and discount the great progress in her life, insinuate yourself into any lasting appreciation of the gifts the Enemy has given her, and let her discontent fester.

From what I know of Martha, I suspect that your best avenue would be to feed her feelings of inadequacy that she has not accomplished more in the way of a profession. These days are particularly easy to accomplish this because she, like so many women, has fallen into the idea that she can be all things to all people; the superwoman, in the parlance of the day. Let her take for granted and minimize the gifts of life and nurturance she has brought to her children. Let her underestimate how much help she has truly given to her husband in his own spiritual path and development. Let her devalue, as much as possible, her genuine caring for other human beings. Feed her discontent that she has not become a career woman and a perfect mother and an exemplary wife all at the same time. Let her imagine what her life might have been had she not chosen marriage and family as she did, and always, always, make the imaginings more glamorous than we know them to be in reality.

If you agitate her discontent with herself (it is often remarkably easy to do so for years with very little effort on your part), then we will have accomplished much in the way of our goal. Despite the fact that the Creator loves these imbeciles just as they are and wants only their best for His eternity, they rarely understand this and seldom appreciate it. It is amusing, is it not, that He knows all their flaws and brokenness and loves them fully, while they barely understand themselves at all and can accept so little of what they are?

Sincerely,
Screwtape

Letter 25

Dear Rotbranch,

Your last letter proves that much of our training has been wasted on you. You give up far too easily, and persist in taking temporary setback as final failure. You might as well be human.

Your loathsome wailing that Peter has now been sober for almost three months is unprecedented by any protégé of mine. Instead of viewing this as an opportunity, you are simply ready to give him up to the Enemy. How dare you! Allow me, once again, to refresh your obviously impaired memory.

Peter's efforts to quit drinking have been successful up to this point. You are correct to be concerned that he is going to recovery meetings. You are also correct to be disturbed that he is praying and is trying to get better day by day. These changes are undoubtedly cause for joy to God and therefore anathema to us; however, they do not represent a final loss. How many, many times did your instructors repeat the admonition to twist humans to our ends, wherever they are? Your opportunity to afflict his spirit will soon be found in his very success! How could you have forgotten this most basic of lessons?

Soon, if not already, Peter will be feeling more and more *self*-confident, more able to control his own life, more convinced that he can be a normal drinker after all. In short, you will soon be able to lead him to forget that it was the Enemy that has given him the gift of sobriety and the Grace to get where he is today. If he remembers at all, lead him to experience the memory as vague and listless, a lifeless thought that means nothing to his transformation. Alcoholics have incredibly short memories when it comes to their failed attempts to give up drinking on their own and, lured by the strength of the disease, are prone to block any truthful recall of their former hopelessness.

Lead him into the temptation to feel pride in himself and his successes in not drinking. Very soon he will have convinced himself that *he* can control it if *he* is careful. His recent success can be twisted to become the very seed of his return to alcohol, if you work him correctly. Alcoholics have no natural defense against the first thought to have a drink. Select an opportune time when Peter is hungry, angry, lonely or tired. These conditions weaken the defenses of most mortals and make them more vulnerable to your suggestion. At such times he is far less likely to use the defensive tools he has acquired in recovery, and therefore more likely to follow the foul and self-destructive path you have laid out for him.

You probably will have to divert his attention from recovery meetings. If you cannot prevent his going, at least nurture his return to dishonesty and deception. Let him tell no one that he is starting to feel so good that he thinks maybe he can start drinking again. Let him avoid any honest exchanges with his sponsor, who would quickly confront him with the truth. Lead Peter to see himself as different from those other fellows, stronger and smarter. Plant the idea in his mind that he has learned enough about himself to be able to avoid the same mistakes he made in the past! Since Peter had always been a binge drinker and rarely overconsumed between bouts, lead him to think that he can control his drinking if only he drinks a little daily instead of a lot sporadically. Above all, blind him to the truth that his disease, although now in check, is distorting his judgment and leading him to believe the lie.

Like most humans, Peter wants to be in charge of his own life and is ambivalent about placing himself in God's hands. Now that he is feeling better, he thinks he is quite competent to take over the helm of his life. Blind him to the recollection that this same thinking had only devastating results in the past. He now knows better, of course, deep down, but his denial is not yet healed and you can divert his attention from the real truth. Like most alcoholics, he knows people who have died from the disease either in accidents or through the inevitable physical deterioration. Should any thoughts of these fatalities creep into his mind, remind him that he has better judgment than did they. Like most alcoholics, he knows others who have abandoned recovery and returned to their active addictions, soon becoming far worse than they were earlier. Remind him that these people simply did not learn anything and that he is smarter than they are. Like most alcoholics, he knows many people who lost jobs, homes, or marriages before they ever got into recovery. Let him congratulate himself (not thank the Enemy) that those things had not happened to him, and that must mean that he really is not alcoholic after all. Blind him to the realization that when he stopped drinking, those consequences simply had not happened to him yet. Like most alcoholics, he knows people who ended up in prison or mental hospitals as a result of their drinking. Remind him that he would never go that far if he starts drinking again.

In short, get Peter to believe the lie. There is nothing else you have to do. Only the Truth will make them free.

I urge you at this point to work particularly toward disrupting his prayer life. Your reports indicate that his prayer has already become more and more lukewarm, a very positive sign for us. Now that things are going better, let his prayers be distracted and empty. With your help, he has almost completely forgotten the lessons he learned months ago about humility. Next to honesty, there is no more formidable barrier to our work. Continue gnawing away at any tendencies he might have to either of these qualities. You will then achieve much greater success in aborting heartfelt prayer. It is no loss to us if he continues saying prayers, mouthing words that he learned as a child or at church or those damnable recovery meetings. Just be sure that whatever he is saying is coming from his memory, rather than his heart.

When Peter's earlier pain became too great to bear, he had little choice but to humble himself and ask for help. Having spent considerable time on the floor when drinking, he didn't have far to move to his knees in prayer for rescue. Now that he is *self*-confident and standing tall in his own mind, humility is slipping away and he has to lower himself to get down on his knees to pray. For some humans, prayer posture makes no difference. Peter is not of this sort. Nor is he of the sort, relatively rare among mortals, who can live their daily activities as prayer. No, his type is one who says prayers; he approaches this as a mental activity to do rather than a way of living. There is thus almost no chance that his prayer life will take another route as you divert any real humility. Once this quality is safely barren, your dissolution of his honesty will proceed much more rapidly. I predict that following this course will lead him to resume drinking again in a matter of weeks.

Let me reiterate my earlier point: save for God's intervention, you can turn any human success into an opening for our torments.

Sincerely,
Screwtape

Letter 26

Dear Rotbranch,

One thing only is necessary for us to win: despair! It is of great concern to me that you appear to have relaxed after your recent victory over Sarah. You carefully led her to this point and cultivated her hopelessness quite well. I applaud you for this achievement, but curse you for resting and taking so much delight in your own ravenous accomplishment. Fool! Have you forgotten that the Enemy is ever ready to intervene? You have not won a permanent victory and I fear that even now His cursed hand is at work to lead her out of your grip.

Have you not noticed that she is being supported in small ways, that comfort is coming to her from sources that she would not have predicted or expected? Have you become so swollen by your triumph that you cannot see the potential destruction of our efforts that simple compassion might bring? Have you forgotten your earliest fiendish drills to be ever wary of the small turning points?

Your predecessor had also become careless. Thinking that Sarah was safely within our gloom due to her agnosticism, inadequate attention was paid to her movement toward recovery. I need not remind you that your predecessor is gone. Sarah probably could have been diverted from recovery, but was not. When she entered AA, it was out of desperation; she had no beliefs in Him or much else in her life. She was convinced that the program could not, would not, work for her because she lacked any belief in a Higher Power or God or anything that might help lift her out of her misery. She was determined to hang onto her old beliefs. Your predecessor should have capitalized on her agnosticism and led her away from recovery, but had become bloated by earlier successes. Little by little, Sarah started noticing that others had what she did not, a belief in something greater than herself, a belief which gave them joy and serenity beyond any she had ever known. How could she not be drawn to this? Perhaps your predecessor could still have saved the day for us, but failed. I yet remember the moment when the tiniest seed of possibility took root in her heart with her recognition that maybe, after all her denial and refusal, there might be a God in the universe. Once she opened to the possibility. . . . well, you know the rest. It was a foul, foul hour that she first believed.

Sarah is inclined to look for another big miracle in her life, a sweeping gesture from her new God that what she wants will be granted. She wants, deep within her heart, her children to be just as she would have them, her husband to become suddenly saintlike in his patience, and her boss to fully appreciate all of her efforts. With your help she will want all the glory of the resurrection, without any cross to carry along the way. Since this will not happen in her life, you can continue to erode her fragile faith with despair.

If you fail to maintain her in this state of despair, you will have an even harder job with her the next time we need part of her soul for our appetite. Above all, you must keep gratitude far from her heart. Since the revolutionary miracles she so desires are unlikely to occur, you must blind her to any gratefulness for the small blessings in life. Small gratitudes have a way of taking root and growing in the receptive human heart, and are always ruinous to our needs.

Should someone compliment her on how well she looks, you must immediately plant the fear that people appreciate her only for her appearance. Should one of the children do something unexpectedly kind, you must intrude upon her thoughts the cynicism that they have often disappointed her in the past. If her boss favorably comments on something she has done, you must plant the seed of suspicion that she will soon be asked to do something she does not want to do. In short, blind her to the little things which might help lead her out of her moroseness. Let her accept nothing into her heart which might stir a response of soul-felt gratitude.

I trust that this is starting to refresh your memory. The Enemy is inclined to speak to these creatures in whispers, in small doings which they have the habit of missing (with our help, of course). A cool breeze across her cheek, a moment of peace during a hectic day, a melody which stirs a happy memory—these small things can all be fodder for humans to feel gratitude. Always, always abort this; gratitude is the enemy of despair. We need not worry that many of them will truly practice gratitude as a daily thanksgiving; let them save it for only special moments when their feelings are already stirred by something else. How much more difficult our work would be if they had the slightest recognition of how much in their lives is Godsend.

Keep Sarah trapped within herself. Make her feelings so fetid that she wants nothing to do with anyone else. You have been quite successful in diverting her intent to go back to recovery meetings; continue your cunning work. If she should have any thought that she might help another, remind her that no one would want to talk to her when she feels so miserable. Divert any resolve to share her despair with another. The simple act of sharing enables human communion to occur. In communion there is always the possibility that they will find Him, ready to do for them what they cannot do for themselves.

Aggravate her thinking so that what could be an emotional molehill becomes a mountain of despair. When she interacts with others at work, at home or in other matters of daily life, let her notice how well everyone else seems to be doing. Let her perceive and magnify their apparent contentment. If you have successfully blinded her, she will not realize that she is comparing how she feels inside with what she perceives others to feel based on their outsides. The gain for us here is obvious. Already besieged by despair, the apparent contentment of others will exacerbate her own suffering. Among mortals, misery does, indeed, love company. With some careful guidance on your part, you can lead her to others who are also despairing or are, at least, quite down on life. They can then reinfect each other with mutual discontent and further the evil you began.

You have all the tools you need at your disposal. There can be no excuse for any failure in this matter! As you know, the Enemy sends His angels in human form to console every suffering soul. It is your task to maintain their blindness, and by so doing make them impotent to acknowledge the quiet workings of human angels. While it is true that only the Enemy can give them a grateful heart, an act of will is required on their part; they must be open to the possibility.

Sincerely,
Screwtape

Letter 27

Dear Rotbranch,

Your last letter interested me; an unusual reaction on my part, as I usually know what there is to know about mortals. I inquired of our research division and they confirmed that some humans are born with the tendency to worry; it seems to have something to do with a chemical imbalance that leads them to become obsessed or preoccupied with their thoughts. While most people can simply turn to other matters of thought with relative ease, some—afflicted with this imbalance—become almost trapped within their thoughts. Only He knows why some humans have this tendency to mental quicksand, and it is unlikely that the reason will ever be revealed to us. However, the absence of reason has never been a handicap to us before, nor should it be now.

Your assessment of the situation is correct. Some with the disease of alcoholism are more prone to worry and obsession than others. For them (although not necessarily for other mortals), worry is tied into their needs to control, to know the future, to be in charge. Your task is clear. Aggravate those who are prone to worry and cause as much trouble as you can for those who are not. As you have already noticed, many mortals spend much of their time worrying about the past and the future. Anytime we can lead them out of the present moment our opportunities for affliction are multiplied. It seems to mean little to them that the Son taught them about the "birds of the field"; they don't truly practice most of their religious beliefs anyway. Nor does it matter much that their worrying accomplishes nothing and only serves to keep them in a state of unrest. With your help, the unrest can be utilized for our purposes.

It is to our advantage to blind humans to the contradiction between worrying and praying, and any number of them—most in fact—will live their entire lives without this recognition (if we are persistent). If they are praying to the cursed Creator, then they are asking His intervention, putting the matter into His hands, turning it over to Him. If they are worrying about the same matter, it is as if they really do not trust Him to have heard their prayers or to be concerned with their needs. It is your job to keep them in the darkness about this. If they are praying, they are wasting their time worrying, and if they are worrying, they are wasting their time praying. Let them do both; the hypocrisy and inherent distrust amuse me!

Even those of great faith, who are often otherwise resistant to our influences, can be led down our path through the disruption of worry. Your task is to lead them into carefully constructed obsession—but not so intense that it alarms their healthier side. Those in recovery programs are encouraged to live one day at a time. This is, I am loathe to admit, a formidable barrier against the particular temptation to worry. The best avenue to pursue is through their need to plan. Lead them to confuse prediction with responsibility and planning.

Humans in many cultures have developed a planning mentality which, by its very excess, is superbly crafted for our purposes. In the interest of what the puny creatures call goals and objectives, they often try to plan their lives as they might the assembly of a child's toy. The planning efforts themselves do not help us that much. However, where you and your colleagues can best disrupt their lives is through their depending on the fulfillment of their plans. Let them envision the results of their plan and, as they attempt to make the desired result a reality, try to bend others to their will to assure their own success. They will rationalize that all they are doing is being conscientious, when you have led them once again to be controlling and manipulative. Never, ever, underestimate the power of selfish interests! (Many of those in recovery programs have learned that it is fine to plan, but dangerous to count on the results. These mortals are a tougher target for our seductions, but by no means impervious).

Once people start counting on results, you have great opportunity to wreak havoc in their lives. They will come to feel entitled to achieving their plans, and cheated if something goes wrong. Lead them to forget that it was, after all, just a plan. Mortals become wed to their plans and the outcomes they want. Anything which disrupts their plans is taken as an affront—just because they devised the plan, if you can imagine! One avenue for you is to strengthen their fantasies of what it will be like when the plan is achieved, thereby causing no small amount of turmoil when anything happens to delay or divert what they had wanted. Since very little will actually happen the way it is planned—with or without your intervention—your chances for aggravating the inclination to worry are excellent.

Gradually lead them into a state of mind where their thinking becomes more and more dominated by what they want to achieve in the future. Tempt them to worry about what can go wrong. The energy they spend in worrying will then invest the whole plan with a significance which it did not originally possess, but this transformation will be beyond their realization. The power of worry will distort their perspectives and help entrap them in a state of agitation, most of it borrowed from the future. If their plan does not come to fruition, you then have additional opportunities for nurturing resentment.

I need not remind you that the Enemy constantly helps these mortal fools in their daily lives, not particularly by giving them what they want, but always providing what they need. Trapping them in their future wants and blinding them to their present needs provides great leverage for us. Many of them will complain bitterly that His help is poorly-timed; we know, curse Him, that it is always, always, on time. His, not theirs.

Many alcoholics are very much all-or-none people, and even those in recovery seldom lose this quality entirely. Tempt them to live at the extremes: over-planning (and over-worry) or no planning at all. It is a special amusement for me to see those mortals who have turned their will and lives over to the care of God—and then do absolutely nothing to help themselves. One of theirs once said that "faith may move mountains, but it helps to take your shovel." Fortunately for us, few humans have any recognition of this; with your help they will forget both their faith and their shovels.

Sincerely,
Screwtape

Letter 28

Dear Rotbranch,

Your bungling of Lydia's case should cost you your miserable existence, and well could have were it not for my intervention with Lucifer. He was eager to dispense with you forever, but I pled your case and convinced him on the grounds that you might still fatten yourself on the rot of some soul.

Fool! For 20 years your predecessors had carefully nurtured Lydia's resentments, never allowing them to die nor inflaming them into hatreds. We knew that if she became too inflamed she would become alerted and, realizing what she had become, take action to change. Misfit! What could you have been thinking in allowing her to erupt in a rage? Now, much work has been undone and reclaiming our previous gains will be formidable.

The Enemy loves these humans whatever they are, although He doesn't seem to want them to be lukewarm. It is always, always to our advantage to help keep their beliefs and emotions tepid. This is nowhere more true than with the normal human dislikes and disappointments. People, places and things can always be manipulated to our purposes—to arouse their resentments and keep them in a chronic state of agitation. He wants them to think of each other as sisters and brothers, and to love one another as He loves them. Love is really all He wants for them. We simply cannot permit that; judgments and resentments are powerful weapons in our arsenal, and an unforgiving heart should always be nurtured in order to block love.

Every once in awhile you will encounter a human who has learned that feeling anger is unavoidable in life, but that it need not be coddled into resentment. Fortunately for us, such humans are rare. Whenever you have the opportunity, plant the seed of resentment after an impulsive judgment or anger. No human can control their first thoughts; with cunning, we can dominate and poison their following thoughts.

Remind them that the other person had no right to say what they said to them, or do what they did to them; remind them that they are entitled to what they want, that their own choice or direction is always the right one. Insinuate self-righteousness into their thinking. Lead them to the thought that they have been treated unfairly. Any of these ploys can, if carefully nurtured, impede them in forming more loving relationships with their brothers and sisters on earth. At a minimum, their lack of acceptance of people, places or things as they are will keep them in an agitated state. You must particularly embattle those in recovery programs like AA. Those fools teach and believe that acceptance is the answer to all their problems. Unfortunately for us, they are right; and their realization has cost us far too many souls that might otherwise have been feast for our table.

Lydia is human: she wants to be honored, applauded and appreciated for not drinking. She wants the world to be extra considerate of her for the sacrifice she feels she is making. How quickly she has forgotten that sobriety is a gift from Him, and all she has done is to accept the gift. Like most humans she has a selfish side that wants her way, and gets resentful when she doesn't get it. Mortals just love to whine about what they lack, instead of rejoicing for what they have been given. If He were not infinite love and infinite goodness, He would have given up on them eons ago.

To the point. You, and you alone, allowed Lydia's long term resentment against her mother to explode into rage. You could have blocked this and furthered the rot of chronic resentment within her soul. Now, her rage has so alarmed her that she is fully aware of how long these resentments have been eating away at her. She finally understands, thanks to your carelessness, that her resentments have contributed greatly to the antagonistic relationship which they have had for years. We had their relationship perfectly poisoned, each set against the other in her own way. And you, my foolish protégé, have undone all this by allowing the moment of rage which jolted her into self-honesty! Lydia now sees her role in this and is aghast. Her self-righteous judgments of her mother prevented any real love between them for years. Should love be recreated in this relationship, you will have severe penalties to endure. Damn you!

I can quite well guess what is even now taking place. Having thus been alarmed and brought into awareness, Lydia is awake to herself, her real self. She is consciously and prayerfully practicing acceptance of her mother as she is, asking Him everyday for the gift of acceptance. She recognizes the burden which she has been carrying all these years (thanks to our efforts), and is beginning to realize that her mother has done the best she could do. She has even come to see that she was never abandoned by her mother's heart during the worst of her drinking days, and has come to be grateful. Grateful to her mother! It should make you cower. Her gratitude makes all resentments impotent!

Perhaps I should not have intervened on your behalf. You dare not, for the sake of your existence, allow another mistake of this magnitude. While the Enemy in heaven is always forgiving, Our Father Below knows no mercy. I can assure you that his sparing you this time has nothing to do with the slightest care for you. He would enjoy your dissolution. Rather, there is a chance that he will enjoy himself even more should you fatten yourself on a few more souls before your end.

Sincerely,
Screwtape

Letter 29

Dear Rotbranch,

There is much more you could be doing to create hatred, injury, doubt, despair, darkness and sadness. The infernal Creator wants just the opposite, so the path of our affliction is clear.

One of your failures is not being more offensive with those mortals who are in recovery programs. Do not for a moment think that they are beyond our powers. Indeed, people who are in such programs, but not really living them, are wonderfully succulent targets. Human patterns of self-deception do not just disappear when they join a recovery program; if you do your evil carefully, you can blind many of them even while they believe they are doing something. Since those with the disease typically are loathe to change, reinforce their inertia as much as possible. At meetings, lead them to be spectators rather than participants.

It is true, much to the wrath of Our Father Below, that humans who are living the simple principles of their recovery programs make much more difficult targets. As I have told you before, the rise of recovery programs in this century has brought potential calamity for us. Fortunately, relatively few ever see this light, so our work has not been made that much more difficult—yet.

It is still easy enough with those in recovery programs to implant the first thought about having a drink; the disease itself works to our advantage here. Mortals cannot achieve a total imperviousness to such thoughts although, of course, most of them would like to. Our task, as always, is to lead them further into temptation and deliver them into evil. Unfortunately, many of them have learned to combat such "first thoughts" through their recovery wisdom. Having learned to be wary of temptations (at least when it comes to alcohol), they turn too quickly to the Enemy for help, and then to their colleagues in the program. Our efforts are greatly hampered when they expose their temptations and defects to other members or to God; far better for us to encourage their secrecy.

Their tendency will be, quite naturally, to nurture their thoughts: of drinking, of anger, of resentment, of fear, of self-pity, of selfishness. They are human. But, damn them all to our hell, those who are truly serious about recovery often will not do what comes naturally. Instead they will share the temptation with another and seek help. It is particularly enraging to me when they become practiced in turning their will over to the Creator each day, because then our temptations have much more of a struggle to survive the moment. Do not give up.

Some of your classmates have become particularly proficient at the anniversary lesson and you could learn something from them. Perhaps you were not paying sufficient attention when this material was covered, so I will remind you—only once. At a minimum, anniversary efforts provide great sport for us; at best, we may lead some of them back to our path.

Mortals love to commemorate moments of some achievement and attach a special significance to the passing of time. Since we do not experience time as they do, it is difficult to understand this attachment. However, our lack of understanding should never prevent us from using the attachment to anniversaries for our purposes. Those in recovery often mark their progress by time increments: one month or six or a year in recovery, that sort of thing. It is great fun to toy with their thoughts and moods as they approach such anniversary times. Since they almost invariably will want a "special" mood, something fairly exalted to mark the occasion, it is a uniquely opportune time for us to make their lives troublesome or, at a minimum, ordinary. Thus, what they might pass by as all in the flow of things at other times will be vexing and troubling as they approach some anniversary.

You need not try to induce any great crisis or catastrophe; it is often sufficient for our purposes to lead them into a protracted gray period. Discourage any gratitude they might start to feel. Block any true appreciation for how much their lives have changed for the better. Blind any memory of the hopelessness and despair they had when they started into recovery. Whatever is problematic or unresolved in their lives can often be nurtured into great dissatisfaction. Encourage and promote grating thoughts of discontent that they have to continue working at getting better. Make them long for some illusory spiritual plateau where further growth (which they will not recognize as life itself) is unnecessary. Lead them away from any memory that they once truly believed that the end of drinking meant that they would never laugh again, would never know joy or unrestrained exuberance. In short, remind them of the often difficult path of life and, at the same time, dilute any genuine gratitude for how far they have come with His damnable help.

Anniversaries provide this special opportunity to nurture a lack of gratitude because they so much want to feel wonderful, beyond the ordinary, beyond trouble. Knowing that their lives are infinitely better is not enough, they will want to feel the ecstasy at a time on the calendar. As always, the Enemy stands ever ready to help them, even when they cannot find gratitude within their hearts. He delights in their joys, relishes their achievements, and feels their sorrows. Blind them to the fact that, where they once drank the cup of alcohol and despair, their daily bread has become serenity and hope.

Sincerely,
Screwtape

Letter 30

Dear Rotbranch,

You seem to be having trouble with your client in consistently maiming his spirit.

Perhaps I may offer some advice. It is to our great advantage, in both the short and long run, if you can get your client to be angry at the Enemy. Now, as I have cautioned you before, not so angry that he overreacts and runs back into His damnable arms, but chronically low-key angry so that there is always a barrier. At the very least, his prayer life will be interrupted, shallow and dry. That might be enough for lesser devils, but never for us!

Create this barrier and we will have gained a solid foothold. One of our very best strategies, so effective that mortals seldom realize what is happening, is to agitate your client's sense of fairness. These beings want things to be fair! Can you believe that? Little do they realize with their puny brains that a fair life would not be endurable for them, for they would then reap the consequences of their actions instead of being forgiven for eternity by the Enemy. Fair! Hah! They could not withstand it for a day. Fortunately for us, they want fair, which always means—as they see it. It is almost pathetic, if you have done your work right, how fair becomes defined in such subjective and myopic terms that these beings would have the universe conform to their wants. I know, I know, it is bizarre indeed. But, we shall not complain, as it is to our great advantage. You would have thought that some of them might have learned a lesson from the time when He asked his lackey, Job, where he was when He founded the earth.

One of the surest ways to get the beings angry at the Enemy is to lead them to expect quick and obvious answers to their prayers; fast food for the soul, as it were. You and I both know that time does not work for humans as it does for the Enemy, so they have the sense that He is withholding help (defined by their time frame) when He could be giving it so freely. Never mind that He has already made one supreme sacrifice. They have such limited vision that that was all in the past to them, instead of seeing its renewal every day. Lead your client into a mood; within the mood let him start to resent God for not responding more rapidly, and in such conspicuous ways that even his pea brain can understand.

One of my favorite times to plant such seeds is when the humans are in their places of worship. If only it was harder, it would be a more stimulating challenge. As it is, I grew weary of such easy prey eons ago and have since turned that all over to devils in training. You may wish to try it just for your own amusement. Plant the seed that God should have answered by now. Remind him how hard he has been praying, how hard he has been trying to lead the good life. Let him remember and congratulate himself on his struggles to give up drinking. Let him think that he has done his very best and that he deserves an answer to whatever is vexing him. Better yet, let him think that he is entitled to an answer to his questions, a solution to his problems because of his own virtue. I can picture you convulsing in disbelief as you read this, and I know that it is hard to imagine such effrontery.

Humans have very short memories when it serves their purpose, which is for most of their lives. Their purpose! It is part of your task to convince these beings to think that the Enemy should speak to them in words that they can understand just because it happens to suit them to ask, or to pray, or whatever it is they do when they invoke their Creator.

Men are particularly prone to dark moods, and when you can lead a man into himself, and thereby away from the Enemy, you can gain much misery for a very long time. If he starts to remember the gifts bestowed on his life, distract him by a black thought. If he starts to get into a heartfelt prayer, plant a seed of despair. If he starts to laugh at himself for taking himself too seriously, remind him that this is the only life *he* has and *he* has to get it all figured out. In short, lead him to a preoccupation with himself. It is usually not very difficult to do this.

It is also quite amusing to toy with their thoughts when they are in recovery meetings. Although I have enjoined you elsewhere about the danger to us of such programs, do not assume that anyplace is beyond our reach, save Heaven itself. Just as you can torment a mortal in prayer, so too can you afflict their thinking at other times when they least suspect it. If they are in recovery meetings, lead them to compare themselves with others in the most critical of ways. Remind them that they are much better educated than many of those present; remind them that they have never been arrested; remind them that their own lives certainly have not been as disrupted as many. Where they could feel gratitude for such a realization, let them feel judgment. Soon, they will have forgotten why they are there in the first place, and I relish the thought that maybe the angels cringe a little when one of the humans is turned away from gratitude so easily.

Women, too, have their moods, but their rhythmic experience makes them more adept at recognizing and getting out of them. Women are more challenging, I agree, but the victory is all the tastier when we can lead a woman to become angry at the Enemy. They say that we have no fury like a woman scorned. If you can lead one to feel that the Enemy is not listening, is scorning her pleas, you can promote quite atrocious vehemence. I particularly enjoy turning a woman against Him, as He honors them as no mortal ever has.

Sincerely,
Screwtape

Letter 31

Dear Rotbranch,

It puzzles me that at times you excel at the most hideous corruption, but at other times you are a miserably poor tempter. Were you more consistent, you might look forward to a position like mine; the advantages of which are a satisfying banquet of havoc wrought by your fellow tempters. However, I wish this to be a laudatory letter, so let me commend you rather than whet your appetite for a feast which may never be yours.

You have correctly and diabolically encouraged Joanna to isolate herself, and simultaneously fed her belief that she is doing otherwise. If you can maintain her in this limbo, she will grow spiritually more listless and a much more vulnerable target for our interests. Her recovery has proceeded far more smoothly than she expected or believes she deserves, a clear indication that the Enemy is supporting her. Her frequent attendance at AA meetings has convinced her that she is doing what she can do. Your cunning is evident in discouraging her from doing anything more than this. When she has had the thought to go early or stay awhile after a meeting just to socialize with others, you have gently intruded the idea that she really does have so many things to *do*. For as long as possible, keep her as a human doing rather than a human being. When she has had the thought to bring up a problem for discussion, you have reminded her that other peoples' problems are really much worse than her own. When she has had the thought to call her sponsor, you have done well to divert her attention with the idea that it would really be better to have a face-to-face meeting, which she will not get around to doing through your diversions.

I am particularly pleased that you have managed to discourage her from much social interaction of any kind, beyond what is necessary for her to get by. Try to keep her in this state of just getting by for as long as possible. Spare her any great pains. As Joanna becomes more remote from people who genuinely care for her, she not only deprives herself of the good they would bring to her life but has less contact with Him as well. She has not learned that He works through people most of the time. While she might silently admire a beautiful sunset as His handiwork, she is unlikely to realize that the same hand guides people into her life. Let her think of angels only as a remnant of her childish imagination, vaporous things floating around in white doing who knows what. Blind her to any wisdom that He uses ordinary people much of the time to be her angels in times of need. Let her attribute any such human helpfulness to good luck.

Discourage any thoughts she might have about reaching out to help others. She will certainly have these thoughts as her damnable recovery program stresses the importance of "passing it on" to other alcoholics. You can readily abort such helpful thoughts by implanting the idea that she really doesn't know that much, cannot help that much, would not really have that much to say to another. In short, blind her to any realization that even the tiniest help, lovingly given to another human being, is an act of grace and a reflection of the Creator. Keep Joanna in mental darkness about the beginnings of her own recovery. Lead her to forget how much the brief phone calls from another buoyed her hopes. Divert any memory of what it meant to her when, during a painful moment, a compassionate friend reminded her that "this, too, shall pass." Focus her attention on not being able to help that much. She will, of course, want to make an enormous difference in another person's life. Knowing that she is unlikely to be able to do this, you can lead her to do nothing. Let her never suspect that she has already been an angel in others' lives, nor that He might use her often by the simplest acts of good will.

By cutting her off from the myriad possibilities of both giving and receiving, you achieve great potential for producing spiritual languor. Weeks and months will pass by with no awareness on her part of what is happening. Do not discount the great gain of the slow but steady leeching away of her spiritual growth. Keep her from any great pains which might mobilize her into more action.

Isolation is an excellent tool for us because humans are so slow to recognize the spirited doldrums we reap. Even when they become aware of their growing separation from meaningful contact with others they can be discouraged from doing much about it.

It amazes me that they so often wonder how their God can "let" them get into so much pain! They themselves have often made the choices, day by day, which eventually produce the painful situation. Great pain, like great growth, often comes from choices made one day at a time. If Joanna remains isolated long enough, she will certainly fall into another painful spot. Try to keep her precariously balanced: not quite into great pain, but far from any true peace.

God allows His children to have spiritual dry spells along the way of their journey. With a bit of help from us, we can convince them that He is ignoring them. Would that we could be so lucky! They will have these dry spells regardless of what they are doing or not doing in their lives; only He knows why. Since we can never know His heart, we can only deduce that He allows such periods for their own good and growth. And, though this is only speculation, He seems unconcerned that such periods often allow us to produce darkness and discontent. Your job is to intrude yourself into their thinking so we can make the most of their dryness. Let them complain bitterly to Him, let them gradually reduce their prayer life so that little, if anything, is heartfelt. Discourage any thoughts that they might have something to learn from being in a spiritual desert. Keep them distracted with their own dissatisfactions.

With Joanna, as others, you can cause no small amount of low level lethargy by encouraging her isolation; this will diminish any Graces which might be gained in loving interaction with others. Fortunately, we know this and she does not.

Sincerely,
Screwtape

Letter 32

Dear Rotbranch,

Your last letter revealed quite clearly that you are far too tolerant of the mortal quality of humor, apparently believing that there is nothing in this of particular concern to us. How shortsighted and stupid can you be? If you underestimate the benefit of lightheartedness to these fools, you run serious risk of losing them in other ways. Take no chances! Ever.

You must learn to recognize the dangers to us that laughter brings. I am not talking about the laughter that comes at the expense of another, nor the laughter which they might obtain from a ribald joke or two. The humor I am referring to is their sentiment of gladness, of lightness of being, of joy in simple things; these sentiments are despicable and dangerous to our purposes.

Do you not recall your instructions on this? They were quite precise and to the point! As I have reminded you repeatedly, alcoholics want to feel good, all of the time. They will go out of their way to produce (as if they really could) happiness and excitement for themselves; they want the stimulation. They will, if they must, "force" themselves to have fun which, of course, is not really fun at all but the delusion that they are doing what they think they should be doing to have a good time.

In this respect, alcoholics are little different from others who want life or family or friends to entertain them much of the time. Perish the thought that they might be bored for a few moments of their puny lives!

We can usually count on the disease to lead them into despair as their lives become more and more out of control. For active alcoholics, there is little you need do to prevent lightness of spirit; their emotional and spiritual deterioration will largely take care of that for you.

Recovering alcoholics are a quite different menu and you must be far more offensive in killing their tendencies toward joy. There are countless examples of these mortals going into an AA meeting with the heaviest of hearts and, for whatever benevolent and disgusting reasons He has, emerging an hour later laughing and joyful. They even learn to laugh at themselves, and to convert their pains into amusements. Loathsome! Despicable! Whenever this happens, one of ours has failed!

Thomas is a case in point. Your work with him has been almost unendurably bad and, frankly, I do not know how much longer I shall tolerate your ineptitude. Thomas had been a drinker for years, then a dry drunk for a few years, then a drinker again. We had him quite thoroughly confused about himself and his life, always trying to figure things out on his own and make life happen according to his will. He was blinder than most, thanks to the efforts of your predecessors. Then, when you slipped up and allowed that turning point which brought him to his knees and senses out of despair, he joined AA. I still recall the pleasure I felt with his thought that he would never laugh again, would never know joy or freedom again, would never experience gladness of heart. What a wonderful moment that thought was for us! Unfortunately, his joining AA has changed his life; this is totally to your discredit and it shall not be forgotten. Will never be forgotten!

Thomas now has reclaimed his lightheartedness, found that by surrendering his will to the care of God he no longer has to try to make himself have fun. Fun comes to him! Joyful moments come to him! Laughter and lightness and songs in his heart! Spontaneity and freedom and dancing of his spirit! I can barely write the words, they are so offensive to me! The same man has gone from the bleakness of his disease to genuinely trusting Him to guide his life. Thomas never imagined that the cursed Creator would also guide his life to happiness, unforced and free. The puny mortal never dreamed that God could provide more laughter than he could ever produce for himself.

Our cause with Thomas has suffered irreparable damage because of your carelessness. He fully expected his recovery to be humorless and barren, envisioning a journey through the rest of his life with the same feeble spirit he had when he started his program. If you had kept him there, I might have overlooked your allowing the original turning point. However, you did not! Just as his disease had made him progressively more despondent and reclusive, his recovery has made him progressively more joyful and grateful. The disease was leading him toward death in one form or another; recovery has led him to life. Life in the Spirit! Damn you! Damn you! Damn you!

You certainly have noticed how much progress he has made in living one day at a time, have noticed that he prays more spontaneously, have noticed that he does not keep so much buried inside himself. To be sure, he still has many defects, and will probably always have many of them. But (this is unforgivable) he has once again found Hope, and the consequence of this grace is that there are more moments in his life where his spirit is like a butterfly, dancing and floating from joy to joy. I trust that you are finally beginning to get the picture.

Like most mortals, Thomas never dreamed of asking God for fun or joy or lightness of being. They tend to treat Him as a deity who, if not fearsome, is humorless. Just who do they think created the flitting of the butterfly or the frolic of the kitten or the pure, delighting innocence of a baby's smile—or the very capacity for laughter itself?

Sometimes their ignorance astounds even me; see that you do not surpass their blindness with your carelessness. When they feel joy, they are far too grateful. Some of them have even discovered the secret that gratitude will bring joy to their hearts.

You *must* do everything in your power to block this. Once they have discovered the joy which may be found in Him, they run the risk to us of learning to be grateful even for painful moments; when this happens we have lost almost all opportunity. Your time to learn these lessons is not limitless. If you do not block the joy they find in recovery, you cannot expect help from me.

I remind you that Our Father Below has no capacity for forgiveness.

Sincerely,
Screwtape

He has given life for all its emotions, and those who are addicted have tried to produce only the joyful side, the side where they feel good all the time. We know that this is a rejection of life as it really is, but it is to our advantage to keep them ignorant of this truth for as long as possible. As long as they refuse to accept life they can have little genuine spiritual growth. If nothing else, they have to manipulate so many other people to keep their own lives in a constant state of feeling good that they cause much hurt along the way. The fact that such efforts to feel good all the time are inevitably fruitless escapes many of them if we have done our work well.

When they are in recovery, you have multiple opportunities to overwhelm them with their feelings; men, in particular, are vulnerable since they usually have far less knowledge and experience with their own real feelings than do women. If properly manipulated, we can get people to futilely try to control their own feelings in much the same way they attempted to control their drinking for so many years. The strategy is really quite simple: locate the thought that creates within them the most pain and inflame it into despair. We can almost always win something when humans despair.

You had succeeded quite well with Paul in reinforcing his guilt feelings about a difficult choice, had made him fearful that he could ever make a right decision, filled him with doubt that his life would ever be joyful. You had even succeeded in getting him to doubt that his life was really worth living or that the pain was bearable. When he called upon his little mottos about "this too shall pass," and living "one day at a time," you effectively countered this with his paralyzing fears that he had ruined other peoples lives (as if he had the power!). You played him very well, and were able to encourage him to borrow much pain from an unknown future.

Then, my dear Rotbranch, you made your mistake. You must have assumed that he was safely within your grasp, mired in fear and guilt and despair. Did you somehow conclude that one little prayer would not hurt? Did you not notice him sink to his knees and lift his trembling and broken heart to God? Did you think that this effort was too puny to be heard? Fool! You had him right on the edge and let him be snatched to safety!

He could have been ours!

The Creator is always with them. Always. All he had to do was whisper that one pathetic plea for help, and instantly He responded. Don't bother blathering about how Paul still felt miserable. He made the turn out of his own will and powerlessness, and that turn was enough. Is always enough.

Were you so blinded by your own success that you forgot that He will allow his creatures to suffer but never will give them more than they can bear? Humans having alcoholism can often be led to feel that they can (and should be able to) handle anything. They quickly forget that He has carried them countless times. The One who calmed the wind and the sea when His disciples were afraid is equally ready to calm the storm of their hearts. Paul's despair was almost ready for our complete capture until that slight prayer undid all of your efforts. Recovering alcoholics come to learn that they are as powerless over their emotions as they were over their drinking, and woe to us when they start making heartfelt pleas to God for help. Permitting him to get down on his knees was an unforgivable mistake; his own wretchedness brought him to humility and our cause was then lost. I do not have to see what happened. I know. God intervened, provided a breath of hope, a light through the dark tunnel of his torment; once again, we were vanquished by His amazing grace. Paul came into His presence.

I know that you did the best you could and that it is sometimes difficult to utilize just the right strategy. You no doubt genuinely believed that he was firmly within our grasp. Quite possibly you could have led him to suicide or back to the bottle, but no matter. You have many more opportunities, both with him and others, to perfect your skills and contribute to the rot of their souls. Paul will certainly have other times of crisis in his life and, even though he will have learned from this one (which will make your job harder), he will never be perfect.

Continue your work in bringing these mortals to Our Father Below. A single soul lost to the Creator is cause for rejoicing.

Sincerely,
Screwtape

Epilogue

A SHORT MOMENT AFTER ROTBRANCH HAD FINISHED READING the last letter from Screwtape, he simply disappeared from the heart of creation. A human observer would have noticed nothing; there was no sound nor shift in the physical universe. Angels, who notice such things, might have had cause to rejoice were it not for the subsequent ravening.

Seven archdevils, secretly dispatched by Screwtape at the same time he sent his final letter, waited silently while Rotbranch fattened himself on the undeserved and tepid praise contained therein. In forgetting the most basic of lessons, that the devil is lie, Rotbranch failed to realize that he had been damned by faint praise. Watching hungrily, fellow evil rejoiced at the downfall of their colleague, for it served to increase their own voracious appetites. Was Rotbranch inept because there was within a streak of good, preventing him from fully exploiting and using the humans assigned to his destructive purpose? That is not for us to know.

Good expands and nurtures other good, rejoices in that which adds to the love of the Creator. Evil is destructive, consuming, reducing. The point is nothing but itself, its own existence; it is the black hole of soul.

The tender hearted may find some satisfaction in knowing that Rotbranch felt nothing in his ultimate end as he was consumed by the archdevils. He simply no longer was.